The Healthy

CHAR GRILLER

GRILL & SMOKER

COOKBOOK

250 DELICIOUS AND HEALTHY RECIPES TO IMPRESS YOUR FRIENDS AND FAMILY

JANE INGRAM

CONTENTS

INTRODUCTION

How the Char Griller Wood Pellet Grill Works

Essentially, pellet grills are high-performing outdoor cookers that combine elements from smokers, ovens and charcoal or gas grills. They run on 100 per cent hardwood pellets and can provide direct and indirect heat to your grilling.

The hardwood pellets are poured into a storage container, or hopper, in the grill that moves them into a cooking chamber. Through combustion, the pellets ignite and heat the cooking chamber. Fans bring in air which is dispersed throughout the cooking area. You'll want to be sure you can position your grill near an electrical outlet, as these functions are powered by electricity.

Much like an oven, these grills are capable of tracking precise temperatures. You can control these digitally or with a dial to ensure your food is cooked just the way you want.

Wood pellet grills pack a big flavour and allow users better temperature management than traditional grills. You also have the added benefit of choosing the wood you use to grill with — a factor that can impact flavour, cooking time, and maintenance.

Five Significant Reasons to Choose the Char Griller Wood Pellet Grill

1. TASTE

If the taste of your food is one of the most important reasons that you grill, then BBQ pellets should be your first choice. They provide a much better flavor than charcoal, especially when charcoal burners use lighter fluid to start then coals. When you grill with wood pellets, you give your food a strong, smoky flavor. There is also a lower chance of overcooking using a wood pellet grill, and it locks more of the natural moisture into the meat or fish.

Americans are very familiar with the taste and flavor of charcoal. However, when given a chance to barbecue with wood pellets, they find the food is delicious and tender, and it's hard to beat that wonderful flavor.

2. CONVENIENCE AND EASE-OF-USE

When you grill with charcoal, it can be a pain to start and once started it requires your constant attention because you don't want your food to burn or the charcoal to flare up too much. When you use a wood pellet grill, you push a button to start then set your temperature where you know it will give you the flavor that you want and the tenderness that you desire. You can leave the grill and prepare other food that you may be serving at your barbecue. A wood pellet grill burns with consistent heat, so you never have to worry about the grill getting too hot or the wood pellets flaring up and burning your meat or fish, making it tough and unpleasant.

3.   VERSATILITY

When you buy a wood pellet grill, it's like you're getting a smoker for free. You can use your wood pellet grill to barbecue, grill, roast, bake, smoke, and even sear. That's because the ability of a wood pellet grill to cook your food at a consistent temperature allows you to use all these different methods.

Most charcoal grills will smoke, barbecue, grill, and sear and that's about it. Charcoal grills lack the versatility of a wood pellet grill. This is especially important if you like to experiment with your barbecue and use it for cooking in a variety of ways.

4.   SAFETY

With a charcoal grill, even when you're finished grilling, you still need to keep an eye on the hot coals. When you use a wood pellet grill, you simply turn the grill off, and there are no more concerns or wasted fuel.

5.   COST

It would be foolish to say that you can't get a charcoal grill for a reasonable price. Small grills sell for as little as $30. But most people prefer larger grills. In the past, wood pellet grills were more expensive than charcoal grills. But with the advances in technology made by wood pellet grills, along with competition, the costs are relatively similar. The actual difference in price depends on which model you choose. For instance, you can buy a pellet grill where you could use your smartphone to control the temperature.

Then there's the question of fuel. Lump charcoal is relatively inexpensive, but if you barbecue frequently, the cost of charcoal adds up quickly. If, on the other hand, you purchase a 20-pound bag of wood pellets, it can last five times longer than a comparable bag of charcoal because wood pellets burn more slowly.

Tips for Making the Most of Your Char Griller Wood Pellet Grill

(1) Take time to give your grill behind-the-scenes TLC. A clean smoker grill produces flavorful recipes without any lingering oiliness or staleness. We know cleaning's not exactly as fun as whipping up award-winning ribs or deep dish pizzas. Still, it's a necessary component to owning a smoker grill that's going to serve up mouthwatering meals.

(2) Store your wood pellets properly. Wood pellets that have been exposed to humid conditions won't give you the burn you need. Plus, they'll lose their freshness. So keep your wood pellets safe and dry.

(3) Pick the right wood pellet for the job. Want a nice smoke ring around your beef brisket? Choose cherry wood pellets for a predictable presentation. Want strong smoke flavor that stands out? Choose hickory or apple wood pellets for their intensity.

(4) Remember to cold smoke, too. At low temperatures, you can cold smoke foods like cheese, fish, cream and even butter, infusing them with the flavor of food-grade wood pellets made from hardwoods like pecan and oak. Get creative and go the distance by cold smoking ingredients to liven up your cooking.

Tips and Tricks on Cleaning Your Char Griller Wood Pellet Grill

1.   Make sure the grill is cold.
2.   Place the grill rack and the chimney dome in the hot soapy water.
3.   Remove foil from the drip pan and flame reflector and brush off debris; put these parts in the tub only if they're still very dirty after brushing.
4.   Remove solids from the grease bucket and place in the tub.
5.   Scrub all parts, then air-dry completely.
6.   Use the paint stirring stick to clear the grease chute.
7.   Use rubber bands to secure the scrubby to the end of the spoon, brush handle or stirring stick and wipe the (often surprisingly disgusting) inside of the chimney.
8.   Give the inside of the lid a good scrape with the brush.
9.   Vacuum the grill interior and the firepot, being sure to clear the holes in the firepot.
10. Wipe the interior with a scrubby dampened with water or a natural cleaning product.
11. Carefully wipe the temperature probe.
12. Give any stainless steel parts a wipe with stainless steel cleaner.
13. Replace the grease bucket; line it with foil for future easy maintenance.
14. Keep things easy and flavors clean by maintaining your pellet smoker all year. All you'll need: your brass wire brush, a damp rag, and heavy-duty aluminum foil.
15. Run on high for ten minutes, then brush the grates.
16. Switch off and cool the smoker according to your grill's instruction manual.
17. Carefully remove the grease bucket and put it out of the reach of animals.
18. Wipe any drips off the grill exterior with a damp rag.
19. Allow to cool overnight and replace the foil on the drip pan.

POULTRY

Turkey Tips

Cooking Time: 3½ Hrs

Ingredients:
- 7-8 lb. turkey breast, cubed
- 1 medium onion, thinly sliced
- Chicken BBQ rub
- BBQ sauce
- 1-2 Tbsp. butter
- Salt and pepper, to taste

Directions:

1. Place turkey in a large roasting pan in an even layer, add BBQ sauce and turn to evenly coat. Allow to marinate for an hour.

2. Pre-heat grill to 230°F. Place pan with turkey on the grill and smoke for 30 minutes per pound or until internal temperature reaches 165°F.

3. While turkey is smoking, place a cast iron skillet on the grill and heat until very hot.

4. Remove turkey from roasting pan and add to skillet with onions, butter and more BBQ sauce. Allow to smoke for an additional 25 minutes, stirring occasionally.

Turkey Leg Lollipops

Cooking Time: 1.5 Hrs

Ingredients:
- 4 Large Turkey Legs
- 1/2 Cup Char-Griller Original Rub
- 1 Tbsp Olive Oil
- 3/4 Cup BBQ Sauce of Choice
- 1/4 Cup Apple Juice
- 1 tsp Honey
- 1 tsp Char-Griller Original Rub (For Sauce)

Directions:

1. With your boning knife cut where the turkey meat starts to thin out going towards the joint. Cut all around the bone and use a paper towel to help with the removal of the skin and joint. Tip: You will notice tendons and a little bone that runs parallel to the leg after you have cut it. Make sure to remove these with your boning knife or kitchen shears.

2. Wrap the exposed bones in foil (this will help with presentation).

3. Next, rub the turkey legs down with olive oil and apply seasoning liberally to lollipops. Make sure to get as even as a coat as possible.

4. Get your grill between 325 F and 350 F. Add hickory chunks to give the meat an extra layer of flavor.

5. Once the grill is up to temp put the turkey legs on indirect heat.

6. Start preparing the glaze by combining BBQ sauce, apple juice, honey, and seasoning in a microwavable safe cup. Set aside till it is time to glaze.Tip: Warm your sauce up right before it is time to glaze so that it is smooth and doesn't tack on the meat too heavily.

7. Once your turkey has reached internal temp around 165 F it is time to glaze. Dip each turkey lollipop into the cup with your glaze mixture until you have obtained a nice shine.

8. Quickly put the turkey back on the grill and let the internal temp reach 170 F.

9. Pull the turkey and let rest for 10 minutes before you eat. Enjoy!

Beer Can Roasted Turkey Breast

Cooking Time: 4-5 Hrs

Ingredients:

- Turkey Breast
- Favorite Rub/Seasonings: Blues Hog Sweet & Savory and a 50/50 blend of Coarse Salt & Coarse Pepper.
- Olive Oil
- Char-Griller Grills Beer Can Chicken Rack with Beer Can
- Char-Griller Grills Ceramic Akorn Kamado Charcoal Grill, Smokin' Stone & Drip Pan
- Fuel: Fogo Eucalyptus Lump Charcoal
- Char-Griller Grills Folding Probe

Directions:

1. -pound turkey breast with bones: Trim all loose fat and skin. Place the turkey breast on the Beer Can Chicken Rack Apply olive oil to all the sides of the turkey. Season all sides of the meat with your favorite Char-Griller Rub/Seasonings. Preheat grill/smoker to 250°. Once the grill/smoker is preheated, add the Smokin' Stone & Char-Griller Drip Pan filled with water to the grill/smoker. Remember to use your Char-Griller Grills Probe to take the guess work out your cooking. Place turkey in grill/smoker and smoke until internal temperature 165° is met, roughly takes 4-5 Hours
2. Tip: while smoking, if a spot on the meat/skin gets too much char, place a small piece of foil
3. Over the spot to help prevent that spot from burning/drying out. Rotate in the smoker/grill every 45 minutes and rotate the turkey for even cooking. Remove from the smoker/grill and allow to rest for 15-30 minutes. Slice and enjoy.

Fried Chicken And Corn

Cooking Time: 10 Min

Ingredients:

- 2 C. flour
- 2 oz. corn starch
- 2 oz. paprika
- 1 Tbsp. cinnamon
- Salt & pepper to taste
- 4 ears of corn
- 4 oz. melted unsalted butter
- 1 Tbsp. paprika

Directions:

1. Soak chicken up to 24 hours in buttermilk and hot sauce
2. In a bowl mix corn starch, salt & pepper, cinnamon, and paprika
3. Mix ingredients well
4. Add chicken to mixture and coat thoroughly
5. Once coated, let sit for 30 minutes
6. Heat grill to 375°F
7. In a hot cast iron skillet, add chicken and oil
8. Cook chicken 3-5 minutes per side
9. Soak corn in saltwater for up to 24 hours
10. Boil them in butter water for 10 minutes before adding to grill
11. On a plate, mix paprika, salt, pepper, and melted butter
12. Mix and roll corn and cover with mixture
13. Add to grill and cook for 3-5 minutes

Smoked Carolina Turkey

Ingredients:

- 10-12 lb. turkey
- 3 Tbsp. red pepper flakes
- ¼ C. paprika
- ¼ C. ground mustard

- ½ C. brown sugar
- 2 Tbsp. coarse black pepper
- 2 Tbsp. Kosher salt
- 2 Tbsp. melted butter

Directions:

1. Pour melted butter over turkey, or use marinade injector to inject butter into turkey

2. Mix red pepper flakes, paprika, ground mustard, brown sugar, black pepper and salt in small bowl to create seasoning mix

3. Rub turkey all over with seasoning mix

4. Place turkey on grill over indirect heat at 250°F or use Smokin' Stone

5. Inject turkey with its own juices every other hour

6. Cook time is 1 hour per pound or until turkey reaches internal temp of 165°F

Chicken Teriyaki

Ingredients:

- 1 whole chicken
- 1 C. soy sauce
- ½ C. brown sugar
- ¼ C. mirin
- 2 Tbsp. honey
- 3 Tsp. fresh ginger, grated
- 2 Tsp. sesame oil
- 2 Tsp. minced garlic
- ½ C. water
- ¼ C. cornstarch

Directions:

1. In a blender combine soy sauce, brown sugar, mirin, honey, fresh ginger, sesame oil and minced garlic and blend until well combined to create marinade.

2. Rinse the chicken and pat dry with paper towel. Place chicken breast-side down. Using sharp kitchen shears, cut along both sides of the backbone, beginning at the back end. Set aside the backbone and giblets for stock, if desired.

3. Using a sharp knife, slice the keel bone at the back of the chicken and crack it open.

4. Tip: Remove the bone by placing your fingers under it and sliding it out. Doing this will allow the chicken to lay flat when turned over.

5. Place the chicken in a large resealable storage bag and pour in the marinade from Step 1. Seal the bag, making sure there is no excess air inside, and allow to marinate overnight in the refrigerator.

6. Pre-heat grill to 350°F. Place chicken on the grill, skin side up for the first 30 minutes. After 30 minutes, flip the chicken and grill for another 1½-2 hours. Chicken is done when internal temperature reaches 165°F-170°F.

7. Allow to rest before slicing and serving. Enjoy!

Creole Latin Spatchcock Turkey

Cooking Time: 1-2 Hrs

Ingredients:

- Whole turkey
- Kitchen Scissors & Pairing Knife
- Char-Griller Marinade Injector
- Creole Seasoning: Generous Coating
- Sazón Seasoning: Generous Coating
- Adobo Seasoning
- Garlic Powder
- Onion Powder
- Creole Butter Injectable Marinade (17 Oz)
- Fresh or Dry Cilantro
- Olive Oil
- Turkey Oven Bags
- Bucket Or Cooler
- Char-Griller Grill

Directions:

1. Chop up fresh cilantro and set aside.
2. Remove turkey from bag & remove everything inside the cavity area along with the plastic tie holding the legs. 3.Using kitchen scissors & pairing knife remove the backbone to Spatchcock the turkey. Also trim and remove any access fat & skin.
3. Flip Turkey breast side up & push down on the breast using both hands to help flatten the turkey.
4. Inject turkey with Creole Butter. Use any extra Creole & rub on breast under skin.
5. Generously add olive to the both sides of the turkey.Tip: continue to trim access fat & skin as you go along.
6. Generously season the turkey with Adobo, Sazón, Creole, onion powder & garlic powder. Then sprinkle cilantro 8. Place turkey in turkey/oven bag & place in bucket or cooler. Place in refrigerator & allow the turkey to rest for 12-24 hours. Cooking Directions 1. Remove turkey from bucket/cooler & allow to rest at room temperature for 1-2 hours. 2. Preheat your Char-griller Smoker to 240°. 3. Place turkey in smoker and smoke until the turkey reaches 165° internal temperature. Product tip: use the Char-griller remote thermometer or folding prob thermometer. 4. Check on turkey about every hour & baste turkey with butter & spritz with apple juice. Tip: rotate turkey in different directions to allow even cooking. 5. After turkey reaches 165° internal temperature allow the turkey to rest for a minimum of 25 minutes. Sprinkle additional cilantro. 7. Slice, serve & enjoy.

Grilled Pizza Chicken Wings

Cooking Time: 20 Min

Ingredients:

- 1.5 Lbs Chicken Wings
- 1 Cup Marinara Sauce
- 2 Tsp Garlic Powder
- 1 Tsp Chili Flake
- 1 Tsp Dried Oregano
- 1 Tsp Salt & Pepper
- 1/3 Cup Grated Pecorino
- 2 T Fresh Parsley (Chopped)
- 2 T Olive Oil
- 1/3 cup Pepperoni, (Crispy)

Directions:

1. Preheat Grill to Medium heat, we want to keep heat moderately low so we give the wings a chance to crisp slowly without burning.
2. Toss wings in salt, pepper, and olive oil, transfer to grill and cook over medium-low heat for 10 minutes per side, moving around 1-2 times per side, allowing char marks to form.
3. After you've flipped the wings and they've finished cooking, toss in a large bowl with fresh parsley, grated cheese, and remaining spices.
4. Sprinkle rubbed wings with crispy pepperoni and serve with warm marinara for dunking. Enjoy!

Buffalo Ranch Chicken

Ingredients:

- 24 Oz Greek Yogurt
- 1 Ranch Seasoning Packet
- 5 lbs Chicken Legs

Directions:

1. Combine Greek yogurt and ranch seasoning packet. Add Chicken to mixture and stir, making sure to coat chicken well. Cover and place in

refrigerator for 2 hrs. Preheat grill to 350F. Grill chicken using direct heat until an internal temperature of 165F. Remove chicken and toss in your favorite buffalo sauce. Serve and enjoy!

Chicken Fajitas

Cooking Time: 20 Min

Ingredients:

- 1 lb. chicken breasts, filleted in half
- 1 ½ Tsp. seasoned salt
- 1 ½ Tsp. dried oregano
- 1 ½ Tsp. ground cumin
- 1 Tsp. garlic powder
- ½ Tsp. chili powder
- ½ Tsp. paprika
- 2 Tbsp. lemon juice
- 2 Tbsp. vegetable oil
- 1 onion, thinly sliced
- 1-2 bell peppers, cored, stemmed and thinly sliced
- Pico de Gallo, for serving
- Shredded cheese, for serving
- Tortillas

Directions:

1. Rinse chicken and pat dry with paper towel. Pour dry ingredients, lemon juice and vegetable oil into a large resealable plastic bag, add chicken and gently shake to evenly coat. Marinate for 2–3 hours in the refrigerator, or best overnight. 2. Pre-heat grill to 400°F. Place chicken directly on the grill and sear for 5-7 minutes on each side, flipping halfway through for good sear marks. Chicken is done when internal temperature reaches 165°F. Remove chicken from grill and wrap in foil to keep warm. 3. While chicken is searing, place 1-2 Tbsp. of oil on a heated cast iron fajita pan. Using a heat resistant grill glove, carefully pick up the pan and spread the oil around evenly. Place the onions and peppers on the pan and sauté for 5-7 minutes until softened. 4. Toast tortillas on warming rack for 5 minutes. Unwrap chicken from foil and slice into 1" thick strips.

2. To serve, spoon a layer of Pico de Gallo and cheese on tortilla. Top with a layer of peppers and onions and add chicken. Enjoy!

Pulled Chicken Crunch Wrap Style Burritos

Cooking Time: 10 Min

Ingredients:

- 1 Cup of Pulled Chicken Mixed with Taco Seasoning and Enchilada Sauce
- 2 Large Burrito Sized Tortillas
- 2 Corn Tostadas, Or Tortillas You Crisp In The Oven
- 2 Small flour tortilla
- 1 Cup Shredded Lettuce
- 1/2 Cup Pico De Gallo, Or Chopped Tomatoes
- 1/2 Cup Queso
- 1/2 Cup Shredded Cheese
- 1/2 Cup Sour Cream

Directions:

1. Place large tortilla on a flat surface, add half of the chicken mixture and half of the queso. Top with a tostada and half of the sour cream. Sprinkle on half the lettuce, pico, and shredded cheese, and top with the remaining small tortilla. Fold inward over the small tortilla to close and repeat the same process to finish the second crunch wrap.

2. Preheat Char-Griller Flat Iron Griddle over medium heat. Drizzle with 1 tsp oil, and spread

evenly. Place Crunch Wraps seam side down on the griddle and cook for about 5 minutes until golden brown. Flip, and cook for another 5 minutes until the other side is golden brown. Serve while hot and enjoy!

Creole Latin Spiced Rotisserie Chicken

Ingredients:
- Whole Chicken (Any Size)
- Olive Oil
- Creole Seasoning To Taste
- Sazon To Taste
- Adobo To Taste
- Fresh Parsley Flakes or Fresh Cilantro Flakes
- Kitchen Twine
- 1 Onion (Sliced)
- Char-Griller Grills Super Pro & Rotisserie Kit

Directions:
1. Rinse and pat dry chicken. Trim access fat and skin. Apply coating of olive oil to all sides of the chicken. Add Sazon, Creole and adobo seasonings. Add twine and knot the legs and also the wings over the breast. Add chicken to rotisserie rod and lock in using the rotisserie forks. Then Sprinkle fresh parsley or cilantro flakes on to the chicken. Slice onion and place on to a hook. Heat grill with lump charcoal: When coking over an open fire I don't cook at specific temperature. I begin with an equivalent of a 1/2 chimney full of lump charcoal and monitor the fire by feel. I place the charcoal in the middle of the grill in the back. As the charcoal burns I add pieces as the cook goes along. Place rotisserie chicken in the grill along with the onions. Roast chicken until internal 165°. Remove chicken and

onions from the grill. Allow to rest for 15 minutes. Slice and enjoy!

Turkey-mushroom Burger

Cooking Time: 20 Min

Ingredients:
- 1¼ lb. ground turkey
- 1 large Portobello mushroom cap
- 1 Tbsp. shallot, coarsely chopped
- 3 Tbsp. fresh parsley
- 2 Tbsp. olive oil
- 1 Tsp. Worcestershire sauce
- 8 thin slices white cheddar cheese
- 4 Hamburger buns
- Salt and pepper, to taste
- Avocado slices, for topping
- Condiments of choice

Directions:
1. Pre-heat grill to 375°F. Clean the mushroom cap, remove the gills and cut into 1" pieces. Transfer to a food processor and add the shallot and parsley; pulse until chopped. 2. Combine mushroom mixture, turkey, olive oil, Worcestershire sauce, 1 Tsp. salt, and pepper to taste in a large bowl. Mix by hand until just blended. Divide into 4 balls, and form 1" thick patties. Put on a large plate, cover and refrigerate until firm, about 30 minutes. 3. Grill the patties for 4- 5 minutes on each side, with a quarter turn halfway through for good sear marks. Top each with 2 slices of cheese during the last 3 minutes of cooking and allow cheese to melt. Toast hamburger buns on the grill until lightly browned. Allow burgers to rest for 5 minutes before serving.
2. Serve the turkey burgers on hamburger buns and top with avocado slices and condiments of choice.

Classic Smoked Spatchcocked Turkey

Ingredients:
- 14 Lb Turkey
- Char-Griller Chicken Rub
- Ghee or Butter

Directions:

1. Preheat offset smoker to between 225 and 250.

2. Tip: You can also do use the AKORN with a Smoking Stone.

3. Add mesquite or hickory chunks to Side Fire Box.

4. Place turkey on a cutting board breast-side down.

5. Using a pair of kitchen shears, cut the backbone out of the turkey.

6. Flip the turkey so the breast-side is up and using two hands, press down on the breastbone until you hear it break and the turkey lies flat on the cutting board.

7. Season the inside and the outside of the turkey with Char-Griller Chicken Rub making sure to rub it into the meat.

8. Place a drip pan under the grates where the turkey will sit.

9. Place the turkey on the grates in the middle of the main barrel of the smoker.

10. Baste turkey with melted ghee every 30 to 45 minutes.

11. Add additional lit charcoal if needed to maintain temperature.

12. The turkey is done when a thermometer reads 165 when interested into the thickest part of the breast.

13. Tip: Turkey will take about 30 to 40 minutes per pound to cook.

14. When turkey reaches 165 degrees, remove from grill and let rest for 20 minutes before carving.

Curried Chicken Skewers

Cooking Time: 10-12 Min

Ingredients:
- 3-4 lb. chicken tenders
- 2 Tbsp. vegetable oil
- 2 Tbsp. yellow mustard
- 2 Tbsp. honey
- 2 Tbsp. curry powder
- 1 Tsp. salt
- ½ Tsp. garlic powder
- ½ Tsp. pepper
- ½ Tsp. allspice

Directions:

1. Soak the bamboo skewers in water for 15 minutes, so they don't burn on the grill.

2. While skewers are soaking, rinse the chicken tenders and pat dry with paper towel.

3. Combine oil, mustard, honey, curry powder, garlic powder, allspice, salt and pepper in a medium bowl to make curry seasoning and mix well. Add chicken, turning to coat evenly and skewer.

4. Place skewered chicken tenders on the grill at 375°F for 10 minutes, until internal temperature reaches 165°F.

Flat Iron East Meets West Chicken Fajitas

Cooking Time: Varies Min

Ingredients:

- 6 Chicken Breasts, Cut into Fajita Slices
- 4 Green Peppers, Cut into Slices
- 4 Yellow Peppers, Cut into Slices
- 2 Large Onions, Sliced
- 2 Packs Tortillas
- 2 Eggs
- 2 Tbsp Soy Sauce
- 1 Tbsp Brown Sugar
- 1 tsp Fresh Ginger, Minced
- 2 Cups Cooked Rice
- Sesame Oil
- Sesame Seeds
- 4 Scallions, Sliced
- Char-Griller Chicken Rub
- Salt and Pepper to Taste

Directions:

1. Taking traditional fajita flavors and adding and extra twist to it, you can cook this whole meal on the Flat Iron at one time! Fried rice, marinated chicken, veggies and toasted tortillas all come together to make this great dish.

2. Pre-heat griddle on Medium High

3. Slice chicken breasts into fajita slices

4. Slice peppers, onions, and scallions

5. Mix together soy sauce, brown sugar and ginger. Pour over chicken in bowl and toss to coat

6. Create 4 cooking zones, high, medium high, medium and low

7. Spread sesame oil on griddle

8. Place chicken on high cooking zone and peppers and onions on medium high cooking zone

9. Season peppers and onions with salt and pepper.

10. Place rice on medium cooking zone.

11. Make a circle of oil, crack two eggs into it. Add Char-Griller Chicken Rub to taste and scallions. Scramble eggs.

12. Add eggs to rice and mix well to incorporate. Add more soy sauce to rice if desired.

13. Check on chicken and vegetables. Flip if needed.

14. Place tortillas on low cooking zone to toast.

15. After chicken reaches 165, remove from grill and build fajitas with chicken, peppers, onions, and rice.

16. Garnish with extra scallions and sesame seeds.

Barbecued Turkey

Cooking Time: 4 Hrs

Ingredients:

- 13 lb. turkey, cut into pieces
- 1/2 C. Chicken BBQ rub
- BBQ sauce for brushing

Directions:

1. Season both sides of turkey pieces generously with Chicken BBQ rub, or your favorite rub.

2. Smoke turkey pieces on the grill on direct heat at 225°F for 3 hours and then raise the temperature to 350°F for another hour to finish it off.

3. Brush one side of turkey pieces with BBQ sauce at the 30-minute mark.

4. Flip and brush the other side after 15 minutes. Remove turkey pieces when internal temperature reaches 165°F.

5. Note: The turkey's internal temperature will continue to increase by 5-10 degrees after you pull it off the grill.

Asian Chicken Salad

Cooking Time: 25 Min

Ingredients:

- 4 Cups Mixed Greens
- 2-3 Chicken Breasts
- 1/2 Cup Chopped Carrots
- 1/2 Cup Chopped Cucumber
- 1/2 Cup Chopped Radish
- 1/2 Cup Chopped Cilantro
- 1 Cup Cooked Quinoa
- 1/2 Cup Crispy Wonton Strips
- 1/2 Cup Soy Sauce (Marinade)
- 1/2 Cup Rice Wine Vinegar (Marinade)
- 1/4 Cup Sesame Oil
- 2 Tbsp Chili Garlic Paste or Sriracha
- 2 Tbsp Honey

Directions:

1. Whisk ingredients for marinade and reserve half.

2. Add 2-3 chicken breasts to the remaining marinade and let it sit for at least 30 mins.

3. While your chicken is marinating, preheat your Char-Griller to high heat, scraping your grates to keep your chicken from sticking! Grill chicken for 10-12 mins per side, until inside temp reaches 165. Let rest 10 mins before slicing.

4. Add chicken to a bed of mixed greens with an assortment of veggies the remaining veggies, and pro-tip: I always have a bag of crispy wonton strips in the pantry, so add those for a delicious crunch! Divide the dressing in half and store with the salad for a quick & easy week day lunch!"

Honey Chipotle Chicken Wings

Cooking Time: 15 Min

Ingredients:

- 2 lbs. chicken wings
- 2 oz. apple cider vinegar
- 4 oz. honey
- 2 Tbsp. chipotle pepper
- 2 oz. mustard
- 1-2 Tsp. red pepper flakes
- 4 oz. olive oil
- Salt and pepper to taste

Directions:

1. Mix mustard, red pepper flakes, honey, chipotle peppers, and apple cider vinegar to make chipotle sauce

2. Slowly infuse olive oil slowly while stirring

3. Season with salt and pepper and stir

4. Using only half the sauce, toss the chicken wings in the sauce and set aside the remaining half

5. Place wings on the grill at 350°F, cook for 7-8 minutes

6. Flip wings, and cook another 7-8 minutes

7. Remove wings and toss in the remaining sauce

Chicken Cordon Bleu

Cooking Time: 20 Min

Ingredients:

- 2-3 Chicken breasts
- 6 strips of bacon
- 2 slices deli ham
- 4 slices of cheese
- Jalapeños, seeded and sliced, optional
- Garlic powder
- Salt and pepper, to taste

Directions:

1. Rinse chicken breasts and pat dry with paper towel. Place inside a resealable plastic bag and flatten using a mallet, until about a ½" thick. 2.

Remove chicken from bag and layer a slice of ham and 2 slices of cheese on each. Place jalapeño slices on each, if desired. 3. Tightly roll chicken breast, keeping ham and cheese inside. Wrap each breast with 3 slices of bacon and lightly season with garlic powder, salt and pepper on both sides, to taste. Refrigerate for 10-20 minutes. 4. Pre-heat grill to 400°F and place chicken directly on grates, for about 20 minutes, flipping halfway through for good sear marks. Chicken is done when internal temperature reaches 165°F. 2.   Slice, serve and enjoy!

Grilled Duck Breast

Cooking Time: 20 Min

Ingredients:

- 8 skinned, boned duck breast halves
- ½ Tsp. hot sauce
- 2 Tbsp. minced garlic
- ¼ C. Worcestershire sauce
- ¼ Tsp. black pepper

Directions:

1. Whisk together Worcestershire sauce, olive oil, hot sauce, garlic, and pepper in a large bowl.

2. Rinse duck breasts and pat dry with paper towel. Score the skin of the duck with a sharp knife in a ¼" diamond pattern to render out the fat for crispy skin.

3. Add the duck breasts to bowl and toss well to coat. Cover with plastic wrap and marinate in the refrigerator for 30 minutes or best overnight.

4. Pre-heat grill to 375°F and put an aluminum pan under the grates to catch drippings. Grill the duck, skin side down, for 4-5 minutes per side.

5. Duck is done when internal temperature reaches 135°F for medium-rare. Remove from the grill and allow to rest 5-10 minutes before slicing and serving.

2-burner Flat Iron Seasoned Chicken Breasts

Cooking Time: 20 Min

Ingredients:

- 4 Boneless Chicken Breasts
- 1/4 Cup of Extra Virgin Olive Oil
- 1 Lemon
- 1 Tbsp of Garlic Powder
- 1 Tbsp of Onion Powder
- 1 Tbsp of Italian Seasoning or choice of herbs
- 1 Tbsp of Char-Griller Lemon Pepper Rub
- 1 Tsp of Cayenne Pepper

Directions:

1. If you prefer to rinse your chicken breasts, do so in cold water. Pat completely dry with paper towels. In a resealable bag add olive oil, and all herbs and seasonings. Add chicken and seal the bag before mixing until all pieces are thoroughly coated. Place the bag(s) in the refrigerator for 1 hour-overnight. With Flat Iron preheated to medium heat, add chicken breast and generous squirt of water to the cooktop before covering with the Char-Griller Basting Dome. Keeping covered, allow it to cook for 9-10 minutes. Remove Basting Dome and generously squeeze juice from lemon over each chicken breast. Allow chicken to cook uncovered for 5-6 more minutes, letting water to evaporate and slight crusting to form on bottom before flipping once more. Cook chicken until the internal temperature reaches 165°F. Serve immediately. Enjoy!

Izzy's Cowboy Grillers

Cooking Time: 20 Min

Ingredients:

- 8 Chicken Breasts
- 1 Block Pepper Jack Cheese
- 1 Lb Bacon
- Jalapeño Slices
- All Purpose Seasoning (Pappys Blue Label Is What I Used)

Directions:

1. Slice a pocket in the middle of each chicken breast and place jalapeño slices and a slice of pepper jack cheese inside. Preheat grill to 325F. Wrap each prepared chicken breast in 2 pieces of bacon. Season using your favorite all purpose rub. Grill direct at 325F to an internal temp of 165F. Remove, serve and enjoy!

Garlic Parmesan Chicken Wings

Cooking Time: 45-60 Min

Ingredients:

- 4 lbs. Chicken Wings
- 16oz. bottle Italian dressing
- 1 C. shredded parmesan cheese
- 1/2 Tbsp. onion salt
- 1/2 Tbsp. black pepper
- 1 C. butter
- 1 Tbsp. oregano
- 2 Tbsp. garlic powder
- A pinch of rosemary

Directions:

1. Add charcoal to one side of grill for indirect grilling, or use Smokin' Stone and add flavored wood chips/chunks if desired
2. Let grill preheat to 275°F
3. Place wings on indirect heat side of grill

4. Smoke wings for 45-60 minutes, until internal temp reaches 170°F
5. While wings are smoking, make garlic Parmesan sauce by mixing Parmesan cheese, garlic powder, onion salt, black pepper, butter, oregano and rosemary
6. Remove wings from grill and toss in garlic Parmesan sauce

Bacon Wrapped Chicken Thighs

Cooking Time: 2-3 Hrs

Ingredients:

- 1 Pack of small chicken thighs (remove any excess fat)
- 1 C. Tony Chachere's Creole Seasoning
- 1 lb. smoked bacon
- 1 bottle squeeze butter

Directions:

1. Squirt on a little squeeze butter and spread it over the chicken thigh and the underside of the skin.
2. Replace skin and wrap each thigh in a strip of bacon. Sprinkle lightly with Tony Chachere's Creole Seasoning. Go light as it is very salty.
3. Place on the grill's top rack of the gas grill for 2 hours at 300°F, depending on the size of the thighs it may take a little longer.

Cherry Chipotle Buffalo Wings

Cooking Time: 1 Hrs

Ingredients:

- 4 lbs. chicken wings
- 14 oz. bottle cherry Chipotle BBQ sauce
- 3 Tsp. dried minced onion
- 2 Tsp. Chipotle chili powder
- 1 ½ Tsp. garlic powder
- 1 ½ Tsp. chili powder

- ½ Tsp. smoked paprika
- 2 C. sour cream
- 1 C. blue cheese salad dressing
- 1 C. blue cheese, crumbled
- 1 C. green onions, thinly sliced
- Salt and pepper, to taste

Directions:

1. Combine 1 Tsp rub, sour cream, salad dressing, crumbled blue cheese and green onions together in a medium bowl and mix well. 2. Refrigerate at least 2 hours to blend flavors.

2. Buffalo wings

3. Rinse chicken wings and dry with paper towel. 2. Combine dried minced onion, Chipotle chili powder, garlic powder, chili powder, smoked paprika and salt and pepper, to taste, into a small bowl and mix well. Reserve 1 Tsp. to mix with dipping sauce. Season chicken wings generously with rub. Place wings on the grill, equally spaced in rows, to smoke for 30 minutes when grill temperature reaches 250°F. 4. After letting wings smoke, increase grill temperature to 350°F and cook wings until internal temperature reaches 165°F. 5. Brush on sauce during the last 15 minutes, flipping once and coating evenly every 5 minutes.

Easy Chicken And Cheese Quesadillas

Cooking Time: 10 Min

Ingredients:

- Pack Of Soft Tortillas
- 2 Lbs Chicken Tenderloin
- Your Choice of Cheese
- Your Choice Of Other Toppings

Directions:

1. Bring your griddle to high / medium-high heat, throw down some oil and cook up your chicken. Once they are cooked and chopped up, move them off to the side.

2. Throw down a little more oil because the griddle may be pretty dry by now, then a couple of tortillas to brown and soften up.

3. After flipping the tortillas once, add your toppings. Start with cheese all over the tortillas, then add your other toppings only on one half of the tortilla.

4. Fold the tortilla in half to create your quesadilla. Press firmly to activate the 'cheese glue'.

5. Flip once more to ensure everything is melty goodness inside.

6. Cut with a pizza cutter and serve with your choice of dips!

Beer Soda Can Chicken

Cooking Time: 1.5 Hrs

Ingredients:

- Olive Oil
- Chicken BBQ rub
- Favorite beer/soda

Directions:

1. 4.5 lb whole chicken

2. Cover chicken in olive oil

3. Season the whole chicken on both sides with Chicken BBQ rub, or your favorite poultry rub

4. Open your favorite beer/soda can

5. Place inside the beer can chicken rack

6. Place chicken over the can on the rack

7. Pre-heat grill to 350°F

8. Add Smokin' Stone

9. Place drip pan on Smokin' Stone and add more beer/soda and lemons

10. Cook for about an hour and a half 11. Remove when internal temp reaches 165°F

Chicken Lollipops By Jeremy Souza

Ingredients:

- Chicken Drumsticks
- Favorite Seasoning
- Favorite Sauce or Glaze
- Charcoal
- Smoking Wood Chunks

Directions:

1. Transform the drumsticks into lollipops Using a sharp knife and kitchen shears cut around the chicken ankle to create the handle Remove the skin, meat, tendons, and cartilage to expose the bone. This will be your "lollipop stick" Remove any loose tendons with the kitchen shears To ensure that the chicken legs will stand up straight, flatten the bottoms with a sharp cleaver Cover the chicken leg handles with foil to protect from burning and discoloration Season the chicken liberally with your favorite seasoning. We decided to go with a habanero seasoning to pair with a sweet apricot glaze to come later Preheat your grill or smoker and set it up for 2 Zone Cooking (Direct and Add any smoking chunks or chips at this point if you wish Place the chicken on your grill away from the direct heat and allow to cook and smoke until an internal temperature of 165*F is reached At this point it's time to sauce! Use your favorite sauce and coat each drumstick Return to the smoker and cook for an additional 10 minutes Remove from the smoker and glaze one last time until they're nice and saucy Remove the foil, plate them nicely on a platter and enjoy. These are sure to impress!

Boneless Chicken Thighs Broccolini & Cheesy Potatoes

Cooking Time: 25 Min

Ingredients:

- Boneless Skinless Chicken Thighs
- 4 Large Potatoes
- 1 Small White Onion
- 2 Bundles of Broccolini
- 1 Loaf Garlic Bread
- 1/2 Cup Cheddar Cheese
- Green Onion for Garnish
- Favorite BBQ Rub
- Favorite BBQ Sauce

Directions:

1. First, season chicken thighs on both sides with your favorite BBQ rub
2. Set in fridge while preparing the vegetables
3. Dice potatoes into equal sized pieces
4. Dice onion, combine with potatoes and season with same BBQ rub 5. Wash, clean, and season broccolini with same BBQ rub
5. Fire up the Char-Grillers Triple Play
6. Start cooking potatoes and onions first in a preheated cast iron skillet on the grill
7. Grill chicken thighs over direct heat (Charcoal Side)
8. Char Broccolini over direct heat (Propane Side)
9. Flip chicken once and begin basting with BBQ sauce
10. Once potatoes are fork tender, sprinkle cheddar cheese over top
11. Flip and sauce other side of chicken and remove once an internal temp of 165*F is reached
12. Garnish potatoes with green onion and serve

Smoked Spatchcock Turkey

Cooking Time: 3-4 Hrs

Ingredients:

- 12-20 lb. turkey
- 3/4 C. olive oil
- 3 Tbsp. minced garlic
- 2 Tbsp. fresh rosemary, chopped
- 1 Tbsp. fresh basil, chopped
- 1 Tbsp. Italian seasoning
- 1 Tsp. ground black pepper

Directions:

1. In a small bowl, mix the olive oil, garlic, rosemary, basil, Italian seasoning, black pepper and salt. Set aside. 2. Rinse the turkey inside and out; pat dry. Loosen the skin from the breast. Work it loose to the end of the drumstick being careful not to tear the skin.

2. Tip: This is easily done by slowly working your fingers between the breast and the skin.

3. Using your hand, spread a generous amount of the rosemary mixture under the breast skin and down the thigh and leg. Rub the remainder of the rosemary mixture over the outside of the breast and all over the turkey. 4. Place turkey in your smoker, and smoke at 250°F for 3 to 4 hours, or until the turkey internal temperature reaches a minimum of 165°F.

Spicy Honey Glazed Wings

Cooking Time: 25 Min

Ingredients:

- 3 Lbs Chicken Wings
- A.Vogel Spicy Herbed Sea Salt
- Mikes Hot honey

Directions:

1. Preheat grill to 350F. Season wings with spicy herbed sea salt. Grill wings direct to an internal temperature of 190F. Remove from heat and glaze with Mikes hot honey. Serve and enjoy!

Roasted Spatchcock Turkey

Cooking Time: 45 Min

Ingredients:

- 12-20 lb. Turkey
- 1½ Tsp. rosemary
- 3 Tbsp. Kosher salt
- ¾ Tsp. pepper
- ¾ Tsp. garlic powder

Directions:

1. Combine rosemary, Kosher salt, pepper and garlic powder in a bowl and mix well. Set aside.

2. Rinse the turkey and pat dry with paper towel. Place turkey breast-side down. Using sharp kitchen shears, cut along both sides of the backbone, beginning at the tail end.

3. Tip: Set aside the backbone and giblets for stock, if desired.

4. Open the turkey, remove any large pieces of fat and break the breastbone.

5. Tip: Place your hand on one side of the breast, close to the breastbone, and push down firmly until you hear a crack. Repeat on the other side.

6. Separate the legs and thighs and loosen the skin from the breast and season the meat with herb mixture from Step 1. Do this by slowly working your fingers between the breast and the skin.

7. Generously butter under the skin and on top of the turkey pieces.

8. Place an aluminum pan underneath the grates to catch drippings and juices. Place the breast on the grill first and allow to roast for 20 minutes at

325°F. Collect the juices from the pan and pour into a small bowl for basting.

9. After 20 minutes, add the legs and thighs. Baste the turkey every 25 minutes.

10. Cook until center of breast meat reaches 165°F and skin is golden brown. Remove from grill and let rest 5-10 minutes before slicing and serving.

Smoked Chicken Thighs

Cooking Time: 1 Hrs

Ingredients:

- 7 lbs bone in, skin on chicken quarters
- 1 C. apple cider vinegar
- 1/2 C. extra virgin olive oil
- 1/2 C. extra virgin olive oil
- 1/2 C. minced onion
- 1 1/2 Tsp. kosher salt
- 4 minced garlic cloves

Directions:

1. Mix apple cider vinegar, extra virgin olive oil, minced onion, kosher salt, and garlic cloves in a bowl 2. Pour mixture over chicken.

2. Set in fridge for at least an hour

3. Heat grill to 250°F

4. Add Smokin' Stone 6. Place chicken on grill 7. To crisp up the skin, take temp up to 350°-400°F when chicken has internal temp of 140°F for about 15 minuets 8. Remove chicken when internal temp reaches 165°-185°F

5. Let cool for 10 minutes, then serve.

Grilled Chicken And Broccoli Stir-fry

Cooking Time: 10 Min

Ingredients:

- 1 lb. chicken breast
- 8 oz. bottle Italian dressing
- 1 Tbsp. extra-virgin olive oil
- 1 head broccoli, stemmed and cut into florets
- ½ red pepper, sliced
- ½ green pepper, sliced
- ½ yellow pepper, sliced
- ½ red onion, sliced
- 1 Tbsp. dried basil
- 1 Tbsp. dried oregano
- 1 Tbsp. garlic powder
- Olive oil, for brushing
- Salt and pepper, to taste

Directions:

1. Rinse chicken and pat dry with paper towel. Pour Italian dressing into a large resealable plastic bag, add chicken and gently shake to evenly coat. Marinate for 2–3 hours in the refrigerator, or best overnight.

2. Rinse produce and pat dry with paper towel. Pre-heat grill to 400°F and brush a grill wok with olive oil.

3. Remove chicken from marinade, cut into 1" thick strips and place in grill wok. Discard dressing.

4. Sear the chicken strips evenly on all sides, until golden brown, for about 3 minutes.

5. Add the broccoli, red pepper, green pepper, yellow pepper, and red onion to the wok and cook for about 5 minutes, stirring occasionally.

6. Mix together basil, oregano and garlic powder in a small bowl to make seasoning and add salt and pepper, to taste. Sprinkle over chicken and vegetables and stir to combine.

7. Serve over cooked rice and garnish with fresh basil and chopped cashews or peanuts, if desired.

Creole Hush Puppy Fried Chicken Legs & Thighs

Ingredients:

- 4 Chicken Legs & 4 Thighs
- 2 Cups of Milk
- Garlic Parsley Butter
- CharGriller Creole Seasoning
- Caribeque Lemon Garlic Seasoning
- 2 Tbs of Sazon
- Garlic Powder To Taste
- Black Pepper To Taste
- Crispy Creole Tony Chachere's Hush Puppy 9.5 Oz
- 1 Cup of All Purpose Flour
- 1/2 Cup of Panko Bread Crumbs
- Cayenne Pepper To Taste
- Lard For Frying
- Char-Griller Grills Hybrid Gas and Charcoal Grill With a Side Burner

Directions:

1. Garlic Parsley Buttermilk Prepping
2. In a large bowl add 2 cups Milk Add melted Garlic Parsley Butter: 4 oz. to the milk. -Full Garlic Parsley Recipe links: Written Recipe & Video Recipe Add Char-Griller Grills Lemon Pepper: to taste Add Caribeque Lemon Garlic: to taste Add Black Pepper to Taste Add Garlic powder to Taste Add Creole Seasoning to Taste Mix ingredients thoroughly. Rinse and clean the chicken legs and thighs with cold water and pat dry with a paper towel. Trim any fat or cartilage from the chicken. Place the chicken in the Garlic Parsley Butter Mixture and mix thoroughly. Place in the fridge for 6-24 hours.
3. Batter/Breading Prep
4. In a large pan add the hush puppy mix: 9.5 oz., All Purpose Flour: one cup and Panko Bread Crumbs: ½ cup Add Cayenne Pepper: to taste Add Creole Seasoning: to taste Add Sazon: 2 tbs Add Black Pepper: to taste Mix all the ingredients thoroughly. Remove the chicken from the fridge and bowl. Then place the chicken legs and thighs in the batter/breading. Tip: apply pressure onto the chicken so the batter/breading can be thickly applied to the chicken. Set aside while the cast iron skillet heats up.
5. Cooking Directions
6. Fire up your Char-Griller Grills Hybrid Gas and Charcoal Grill side burner using a large cast iron skillet with lard. Preheat the Cast Iron Skillet with the oil to 335°. Place the chicken into the cast iron skillet for 15 minutes or until internal temperature 175°. Tip: place the chicken thighs skin side down when placing into the cast iron skillet. Remove the chicken from the cast iron skillet and allow it to drain/cool for 7 minutes. Serve and Enjoy

Creole Smokin' Fried Wings

Cooking Time: 1 Hrs

Ingredients:

- 16-20 chicken wings
- 1/2 Tbsp Creole seasoning
- 1/2 Tbsp adobo seasoning
- 1 Tbsp sazón seasoning
- 12 oz. buffalo sauce
- Olive Oil
- All-vegetable shortening

Directions:

1. Coat wings in even layer with olive oil in a large bowl or plastic bag
2. Season with Creole, Adobo & Sazón

3. Place wings in fridge for at least on hour to allow the seasoning to absorb into the wings.

4. Heat grill to 340°F

5. Place wings in grill and smoke with apple wood chunks or your favorite

6. Smoke for 30 mins or until the wings reach internal temp of 140°F

7. Remove wing and place in pan. Set aside pan.

8. Add charcoal to grill and get extremely hot for frying the wings in the cast iron skillet

9. Add all-vegetable shortening to cast iron skillet and then place on grill allowing to heat up

10. Place small batch of wings into skillet and fry for 2-3 minutes or until crispy

11. Remove from skillet and place on baking rack in pan

12. Warm your favorite buffalo sauce

13. Toss wings in warmed buffalo sauce

14. Serve with ranch or blue cheese, carrots, and celery.

Chili Mesquite Lime Shredded Chicken Street Tacos

Cooking Time: 45 Min

Ingredients:

- 6 Tbsp Mesquite Lime Sea Salt
- 2 Tbsp Chili Powder
- 1 Lime (Squeezed)
- 4 Chicken Breasts (Skinless)
- Chili Lime Sauce
- 1 Package Provolone Cheese Slices

Directions:

1. Mix sea salt, powder and lime together Trim any excess fat off chicken breasts Season chicken with sauce and let sit for 10-15 mins Get your grill up to temp at about 400° - 450° Place chicken on grill until IT of 165° Pull chicken and

place in the Instant Pot for 30 mins (add 1/2 cup water) Shred chicken and place on shells, top with pico de gallo and Sriracha Warm up a pan and throw cheese slice in pan When cheese begins to bubble flip over until brown

Garlic Lover's Chicken

Cooking Time: 10 Min

Ingredients:

- 7 lb. whole chicken
- 16 oz. bottle Italian dressing
- 4-5 handfuls peeled garlic cloves, to taste
- 2 Tbsp. butter, melted
- 1 Tsp. olive oil
- 2 Tsp. dried thyme leaves
- 1 Tsp. seasoned salt
- 2 Tsp. white pepper
- 2 Tbsp. flour
- 1 C. low fat milk
- 2 C. dry white wine
- Garlic dry rub or Chicken BBQ rub, to taste

Directions:

1. Rinse chicken, dry with paper towel and cut in half. Marinate chicken halves in Italian dressing for four hours, or overnight. Season generously with garlic dry rub or use Chicken BBQ rub.

2. Roast chicken on the grill at 400°F for 45 minutes. Chicken is done when internal temperature reaches 170°F. Remove chicken from the grill and let rest 5-10 minutes.

3. Garlic sauce

4. Sauté garlic cloves in a medium sauce pan with butter and olive oil until lightly browned. Stir frequently and cook until garlic is soft, 5-7 minutes.

5. Whisk together flour, milk, white wine, thyme and white pepper in a small bowl. Add to garlic, stir to combine and simmer for 10 minutes.
6. To serve, pour garlic sauce over baked chicken halves and enjoy!

Grilled Chicken And Vegetable Kebabs

Cooking Time: 15 Min

Ingredients:

- 2 lbs. boneless, skinless chicken thighs
- 1 C. whole yogurt
- 2 Tbsp. unsalted butter, melted
- 1 Tbsp. salt
- ½ Tsp. ground coriander
- ¼ Tsp. ground turmeric
- Pinch red pepper flakes, optional
- 1 garlic clove, finely grated
- 3 bell peppers, stemmed and cored
- 1 red onion, cut into wedges
- 2 Tbsp. olive oil
- Flatbread, for serving
- Fresh mint and parsley leaves, chopped, for garnish
- Bamboo skewers

Directions:

1. Rinse chicken, pat dry with paper towel and cut into 2" thick pieces. Whisk together yogurt, butter, salt, coriander, turmeric, red pepper flakes and grated garlic in a medium bowl until smooth.
2. Add chicken and toss to evenly coat. Cover bowl with plastic wrap and let marinate at room temperature for 1 hour.
3. Rinse produce. Slice peppers into 2" thick pieces. Toss peppers and onion wedges in a medium bowl with the olive oil, and season with salt, to taste.

4. Soak bamboo skewers in water for 30 minutes. Divide chicken and vegetables evenly between the skewers, alternating between the two.
5. Pre-heat grill to 400°F. Grill kebabs, turning as needed, until the chicken has cooked through, about 15-20 minutes. Chicken is done when internal temperature reaches 165°F.
6. Let rest for 3-5 minutes, then garnish with chopped mint and parsley leaves, and serve with flatbread.
7. Enjoy!

Smoked Turkey Breast

Ingredients:

- 1 Turkey Breast (Thawed)
- 10-12 Cups of cold water
- 1/2 Cup of Kosher Salt
- 1/4 Cup of Brown Sugar
- 1/4 Cup of Extra Virgin Olive Oil
- 1 Tbsp of Chili Powder
- 1 Tbsp of Paprika
- 1 Tbsp of Garlic Powder
- 1 Tbsp of Ground Black pepper
- 1/2 Tbsp of Seasoning Salt

Directions:

1. Mix all the brine ingredients (2-4) in a large container. Submerge the turkey breast and allow it to marinate for 8 hours up to overnight. Remove from the brine and pat dry with paper towels. You may refrigerate for an extra 2 hours to allow skin to completely dry. Preheat your smoker to 225°F. Coat the exterior of your turkey with the olive oil before massaging in the rest of the seasonings and spices ingredients (5-10). Add the turkey to the smoker, breast side up. Smoke until the internal temp reaches about 150°F. This should take about 2 hours. Increase the

temperature to about 500-550°F for about 5 minutes to allow skin to crisp up until the internal temperature reaches 165°F. Allow the turkey to rest for 20-30 minutes before carving. Enjoy!

Gravity 980 Smoked Chicken Wings

Cooking Time: 2.5 Hrs

Ingredients:

- 2 lb. of fresh, thawed Chicken Wings
- 2 Tbsp of Extra Virgin Olive Oil
- 1/4 Cup of Char-Griller Chicken Rub
- 1 Tsp of Cumin
- 1 Tsp of Cayenne Powder

Directions:

1. If you prefer to rinse your chicken wings, do so in cold water. Pat them completely dry with paper towels. In a resealable bag, combine olive oil, and all seasonings, then add chicken and seal bag. Thoroughly mix chicken and oil mixture within bag until all pieces are coated. Place in the refrigerator and allow to sit for 1 hour through overnight. Remove the fire shutter from the Gravity 980, load and light the hopper then set to 225-250°F. Place chicken wings in the grill in a single layer and smoke for 2 to 2 ½ hours or until the internal temperature reaches 165°F. Allow wings to rest for 10-20 minutes then serve. Enjoy!

PIZZA

Flat-iron Pizza Quesadillas

Cooking Time: 10 Min

Ingredients:
- 8 Flour Tortillas
- 1 Pack Of Pepperoni And Or Salami
- 2 Cups Of Mozzarella Cheese
- 4 Tbsp Of Butter Or Margarine
- 2 Cups Of Spaghetti Sauce
- 4 Tbsp Of Dried Basil And Or Oregano

Directions:
1. Heat Flat Iron to medium heat. Add butter to flat top and spread across allowing it to melt. Once heated, place 4 tortillas flat on top. Immediately layer cheese, oregano/basil, meat and more cheese on the tortilla. Top with another tortilla. (Optionally, you can make each tortilla its own mini-quesadilla by only layering meat and cheese on one half then folding it in half.) Allow the cheese to fully melt on the inside before using a spatula to flip each over, adding more butter to the flat top, if necessary. Once cheese is melted and tortillas are browned and crisped to your liking, remove from Flat Iron. Serve each quesadilla with spaghetti sauce for dipping. Enjoy!

Gravity 980 Grilled Pizza

Cooking Time: 12 Min

Ingredients:
- 1 Lb. Fresh Pizza Dough
- 1/4 Cup of Extra Virgin Olive Oil
- All Purpose White Flour
- 1 Cup of Fresh Mozzarella Cheese

- Optional Toppings: Pepperoni, Vegetables, Sausage, Bacon, etc.

Directions:
1. Remove the fire shutter from your Gravity 980, load and light the hopper, then preheat to 500-600°F. Add flour to your counter or cutting board before prepping your dough into the desired pizza shape. Add pizza sauce, olive oil and cheese then add your pizza to the pizza stone. Add any toppings that must be cooked then add to the grill. Cook the pizza for 8-12 minutes or until desired brownness. Add any remaining fresh toppings and serve immediately. Enjoy!

Meat Lovers Pizza

Cooking Time: 9 To 12 Min

Ingredients:
- Pre-made Pizza Dough
- Pizza Sauce
- Garlic Powder - 2 tsp
- Shredded Mozzarella - 1 to 1.5 Cups
- 8 to 10 Slices of Pepperoni
- 1-2 Slices of Ham - Chopped
- 1/2 Cup Spicy Sausage - Browned
- 1/2 Cup Ground Beef - Browned
- Parmesan Cheese - Grated
- 1/2 Cup Arugula
- Olive Oil - 1 Tbs
- Salt and Pepper to Taste

Directions:
1. This Meat Lover's pizza packs on the flavor with ham, spicy sausage, ground beef, pepperoni, and two types of cheese. The optional arugula can take it over the top with its peppery bite. Cook

this hot and fast on the AKORN for restaurant quality crust.

2. Allow pizza dough to come up to room temperature (about 8 hours). Tip: Place Pizza Dough in a large plastic bag that seals for the best results.

3. Brown ground beef and spicy sausage. Set aside.

4. Preheat AKORN to 500-600 degrees Fahrenheit. Insert Smokin' Stone. Place Pizza Stone on grates to heat.

5. Shape dough into pizza on a cutting board covered in semolina.

6. Add desired amount of pizza sauce and garlic powder.

7. Add ground beef and sausage to pizza. Add pepperoni and ham. Add mozzarella cheese.

8. Add parmesan cheese to taste.

9. Place pizza on pizza stone. Close lid and cook for 9 minutes or until crust is crisp and cheese melted.

10. Remove from pizza stone and allow to rest for 5 minutes.

11. Toss arugula with olive oil, salt and pepper.

12. Top pizza with arugula if desired.

Grilled Caprese Pizza

Cooking Time: 6 To 8 Min

Ingredients:

- 1 Ball of Pizza Dough, Rolled out Thinly
- 1/2 Cup Pesto
- 1 Small Ball Fresh Mozzarella, Torn to Shreds
- 1/2 Cup Cherry Tomatoes, Halved
- 4-5 Fresh Basil Leaves, Whole or Torn
- 1 Tbsp Fresh Parsley, Chopped
- 1 Tbsp Fresh Parmesan, Shredded or Grated
- 2 Tbsp Olive Oil
- Salt & Pepper to Taste

Directions:

1. Preheat Char-Griller to high heat. Scrape and oil your grates well so the dough does not stick.

2. Spread 1 T of oil to one side of the dough, and place oiled side down on heat first. Immediately turn burners to low and let dough cook for 2-3 minutes that side, until dough bubbles up.

3. Brush remaining oil on uncooked side, and then carefully use spatula to flip dough over. Turn heat off.

4. Spread the dough evenly with pesto, and scatter the torn mozzarella and halved tomatoes over the top. Close the lid, and allow residual heat from the grill to finish cooking the pizza for 5 minutes.

5. Remove pizza from heat and add fresh basil, parsley, and grated parmesan. Serve while warm. Enjoy!

Fire-grilled Pizza

Cooking Time: 10-15 Min

Ingredients:

- 3 C. bread flour
- 2 Tsp. salt
- 3 Tbsp. vegetable oil
- 1 Tsp. sugar
- 1 packet rapid-rising yeast
- 1 C. water
- Corn meal, for dusting
- Tomato sauce
- Garlic powder
- Cheese, if desired
- Toppings of choice

Directions:

1. In a stand mixer fitted with a dough hook, add water and yeast to the bowl and mix well. Then add sugar, salt and vegetable oil and mix.

2. Add bread flour, 1 C. at a time, and mix until a dough forms. Add water as needed to keep dough from sticking to the sides of the bowl. 3. Remove dough and knead for 1 minute by hand, forming it into a ball. Lightly spray a bowl with cooking spray, add dough ball and lightly spray the top. Cover with plastic wrap and allow dough to rise for 1 hour, until doubled in size.

3. Note: Dough is enough to make 2 medium pizzas. Cut dough in half, wrap unused portion and refrigerate or freeze for later use.

4. Pizza

5. Lightly flour counter. Stretch and work dough by hand, kneading until a 12" circle forms. Transfer dough to a wooden pizza peel lightly dusted with corn meal, to prevent sticking. 2. Pre-heat grill to 450°F. Sprinkle pizza dough with garlic powder. Spoon a layer of tomato sauce in the center and spread around to edges of dough. 3. Sprinkle a layer of cheese on top, if desired. Place other toppings on top of cheese layer. 4. Place pizza on pizza stone and allow pizza to cook for 10-15 minutes with lid closed. Rotate pizza after 5 minutes to ensure even cooking. Remove pizza from grill and allow to rest for 4-5 minutes. Slice and enjoy!

Breakfast Pizza

Cooking Time: 10 To 12 Min

Ingredients:
- Pre-made Pizza Dough
- Sun-dried Tomatoes - 1 Cup
- 1 Fresh Mozzarella Ball
- Deli Ham - 4 slices
- 1 Egg
- 1 (8 oz) Jar Tomato Sauce
- Baby Spinach - 2 Cups
- Dried Basil to Taste
- Salt and Pepper to Taste
- Semolina
- Garlic Powder to Taste

Directions:
1. Allow pre-made pizza dough to sit at room temperature covered with a clean dishcloth for at least 6 hours.
2. Preheat grill to medium high heat
3. Add pizza stone to grill and allow to preheat
4. Spread out pre-made pizza dough on a cutting board covered with semolina
5. Cut up ham and spinach.
6. Cut mozzarella into thin slices
7. Add tomato sauce to pizza. (As much as desired.)
8. Season with Garlic Salt and Basil
9. Add mozzarella slices
10. Add ham, spinach, and sun-dried tomatoes.
11. Add extra semolina to pizza stone and carefully slide pizza on grill.
12. Tip: Have a friend help with this step.
13. Allow to cook for 7 minutes with the lid closed.
14. Open grill and crack one egg onto the pizza.
15. Close the lid and allow to cook for 3 to 4 more minutes or until egg white is opaque.
16. Remove from grill and let rest for 5 minutes.
17. Serve and enjoy

Pepperoni Pizza

Cooking Time: 3-5 Min

Ingredients:

- Pizza Dough/Crust
- Pizza Sauce
- Mozzarella Cheese
- Pepperonis
- Other Toppings

Directions:

1. Add a layer of sauce
2. Spread your favorite toppings
3. Add an even layer of cheese
4. Add more toppings if desired
5. Heat grill to 550°F
6. Place pizza on stone
7. Cook for 3-5 minutes
8. Slice and serve!

Grilled Fathead Pizza

Ingredients:

- 10 oz Shredded Mozzarella Cheese
- 1 Egg
- 5 oz Balanced Almond Flour
- 1 tsp Pizza Seasoning
- 1/3 Cup Marinara Sauce
- 1/2 Pound Ground Italian Sausage, Ground
- 15 Pepperoni Slices
- 1 Green Bell Pepper, Chopped
- 1/2 Red Onion, Chopped
- 1 can sliced black olives
- 1 can sliced mushrooms
- 1.5 Cups Shredded Mozzarella Cheese (Topping)

Directions:

1. Preheat grill to a low temp of about 250°.

2. Melt 10 oz mozzarella cheese in microwave in 30 second increments until all melted, add 1 egg & mix. Once egg is mixed add the almond flour, baking powder & pizza seasoning.

3. Knead with hands until well incorporated (for about 3 minutes).

4. Spread dough out on a baking sheet with parchment paper.

5. Put on grill for about 5-6 minutes until crust is turning golden.

6. Then take crust off the grill, flip over & put back on parchment paper.

7. Add toppings & then put back in the grill for about 10 minutes or until desired doneness.

Pesto Burrata Grilled Pizza

Cooking Time: 3 Min

Ingredients:

- 1 Pizza Dough Ball (Store bought Dough or Homemade Dough)
- 1 Cup pesto
- 1 Cup Fresh Greens (Arugula or Spinach)
- 2 Burrata Balls
- 1/2 Cup Fresh Basil Leaves
- 4 T Olive Oil
- Salt And Pepper To Taste

Directions:

1. Fill chimney with charcoal. Place over side burner and turn flame to high, allowing charcoal to catch fire. If you do not have the side burner on your Texas Trio, you can light paper under the chimney so that it catches. We are cooking on the Akorn Jr today, so prep the base for charcoal, scrape the grates to make sure they're clean, and grab your stone or cast iron for the pizza.

2. Once coals have heated through, about 20 minutes, add them to the base of the Akorn Jr

and place grates over the coals, add cast iron, and close lid to allow grill to heat up.

3. Let's prep the pizza. Cut dough ball into four equal pieces and roll each piece out to a thin circle.

4. I like to plate up all my toppings and take them out to the grill so I can make the pizzas quickly. When it's time- add a drizzle of the olive oil to the stone or cast iron and lay the dough out. Flip after about 60 seconds, once the sides start to golden and you see some bubbles forming. On the now cooked side that is up- spread ¼ cup of the pesto, add half a ball of burrata and close the lid for an additional 1-2 minutes, until the pie is cooked through. Remove from heat and top with arugula, fresh basil leaves, a drizzle of olive oil, and salt and pepper. Repeat three more times until all the pies are done. Serve hot, and enjoy!

Flat Iron Cheesy Pizza Bagels

Cooking Time: 15 Min

Ingredients:

- 3 Bagels Cut in Halves (Whatever type you prefer)

- 1 Can of Pizza Sauce
- 1 Cup of Pepperoni or Salami (Sliced)
- 2 Cups of Mozzarella Cheese
- 2 Tbsp of Butter

Directions:

1. Melt 1 Tbsp of butter on Flat Iron over Medium Heat.

2. Place bagels face down in butter and allow 2-3 minutes for them to lightly toast. Remove from heat.

3. On a separate section of the griddle, warm pepperoni/salami over medium heat for 3-4 minutes then set aside

4. On a tray or large plate, assemble bagel pizzas by spreading each with sauce, then adding desired amount of pepperoni/salami and cheese on top.

5. Place each bagel pizza back on the griddle on another Tbsp of melted butter over on medium-low heat until cheese has thoroughly melted and the bottom is toasted. (It might help to cover each bagel pizza with a basting/grill cover)

6. Serve hot.

SEAFOOD

Honey-bourbon Glazed Salmon

Cooking Time: 45-60 Min

Ingredients:

- 1 Cedar Plank
- 1 Wild Salmon Filet
- 1 Lemon, sliced
- Lemon pepper seasoning (to taste)
- ½ C. Bourbon
- Water (enough to cover the cedar plank)
- 3 Tbsp. Honey
- 1 oz. Bourbon
- 1 Tsp. Lemon Zest

Directions:

1. Remove the pin bones from the salmon filet with fish bone tweezers. Pour water and bourbon into a large baking dish and soak cedar plank for a minimum of 1 hour.

2. Place salmon filet on cedar plank, sprinkle with lemon pepper seasoning, to taste, and cover with sliced lemons.

3. Prepare the grill for offset smoking by adding citrus wood chunks to the Side Fire Box. Place the salmon on the grill and smoke at 250° - 275°F for approximately 45 - 60 minutes.

4. Mix the honey, bourbon and lemon zest together in a bowl to make the glaze. After 30 minutes, intermittently brush the honey/bourbon glaze on the salmon.

5. Enjoy the deliciousness!

Buffalo Lemon Shrimp

Cooking Time: 12 Min

Ingredients:

- Raw Shrimp, Peeled and Deveined - 1 Pound
- Hot Sauce (I Use Buffalo Sauce for this Recipe) - 3 Tablespoons
- Minced Garlic - 1 Tablespoon
- Olive Oil - 2 Tablespoons
- Juiced Lemon - 1
- Lemon Cut Into Wedges for Serving - 1
- Salt to Taste

Directions:

1. Taking advantage of seasonal ingredients is the name of the game, so for the remainder of the summer, chicken wings are going to have to move aside. If you haven't been grilling shrimp this season, now is the time. She loves to use charcoal for this recipe, as shrimp cook quickly and charcoal flame provides so much flavor in such a short amount of time. Let's dig in!

2. Light your charcoal in your chimney and wait until the bricks are glowing red and ashy around the edges. Dump under the grates of your Char-Griller Grill, and close the lid, letting the grates heat for 5-10 minutes.

3. While grill is heating, toss shrimp with buffalo sauce, minced garlic, the juice of one lemon, olive oil, and plenty of salt. Let marinate on the counter for a few minutes.

4. Once the grill is heated, spray the grates with non-stick spray, and lay your shrimp and lemon wedges out to cook. Grill on each side for 2 minutes, until some deep char marks form, and they are curled up and a beautiful vibrant pink color.

5. Serve on a large tray with grilled lemon wedges and an extra sprinkle of salt! These are super delicious on a salad, in a taco, or as the main dish at your next barbecue! Happy Grilling.

Bacon Wrapped Seafood Stuffed Shrimp

Cooking Time: 20 Min

Ingredients:

- 2 lbs. jumbo shrimp, deveined and butterflied
- 1 lb. Applewood smoked bacon strips, cut in half
- 1lb. lobster tail meat and/or lump crab meat, cooked and chopped
- 2 Tbsp. butter, melted
- 1 medium yellow pepper, chopped
- 1 small green pepper, chopped
- 1 medium sweet onion, chopped
- 2 Tbsp. fresh garlic, minced
- ¼ C. mayonnaise
- 1 Tbsp. horseradish mustard
- 1 egg, beaten
- 2 Tbsp. seafood all-purpose sauce
- 1 Tsp. seasoned salt
- 1 Tsp. white pepper
- 1 Tsp. garlic powder
- 1 Tsp. onion powder
- 2 Tsp. Chipotle chili powder
- 1 C. cheese crackers, crushed

Directions:

1. Melt butter in a large cast iron skillet and sauté onion, peppers and garlic until tender, 5-7 minutes.

2. Allow to cool and then gradually fold in the remaining ingredients, except shrimp, to seafood mixture from Step 1.

3. Mound 1-2 Tbsp. of stuffing mixture onto shrimp, wrap with ½ strip of bacon and secure with toothpick.

4. Place bacon wrapped shrimp on a metal tray onto the indirect side of the grill at 375°F for 20 minutes.

Gravity 980 Grilled Lobster Tails

Cooking Time: 10 Min

Ingredients:

- 6 Lobster Tails
- 1/3 Cup of Melted Butter
- 1 Tbsp OF Extra Virgin Olive Oil
- 1 Lemon
- 1 Tbsp of Parsley
- 1 Tbsp of Chives
- 1 Tbsp of Minced Garlic
- 1 Tbsp of Char-Griller Creole Rub
- 1/2 Tsp of Salt
- 1/2 Tsp of Pepper

Directions:

1. To prep lobster tails, using kitchen shears, cut the top of the shell lengthwise down the middle. Using a sharp knife, cut through this slit, halfway through the flesh, excluding the very tip of the tail. Flatten each tail so the shell opens around the meat. Place a skewer through each tail to prevent it from curling during cooking. In a bowl, combine butter, parsley, ½ the chives, minced garlic and Creole rub. Line tails on a baking sheet and brush each lightly with oil, salt and pepper. Remove the fire shutter from your Gravity 980, load and light the hopper then set to 350°F. Place the lobster tails, flesh side down on the grill and allow to cook for 5 minutes. Flip each tail over and drizzle the tops generously with garlic butter mixture. Grill for additional 5 minutes or until lobster becomes fully cooked. Sprinkle finished lobster tails with remaining chives and serve with lemon wedges. Enjoy!

Grilled Swordfish With Lemon-caper Sauce

Ingredients:

- 8oz. swordfish steaks
- 4 oz. jar capers, drained
- ½ C. mayonnaise
- ½ C. sour cream
- 1½ fresh lemons, juiced
- ½ Tsp. seasoned salt
- ¾ Tsp. white pepper
- 1 Tsp. dried minced onion
- 5 Tbsp. green onion tops, minced (optional, for garnish)

Directions:

1. Blend all ingredients, except green onion tops.
2. Transfer to bowl, cover with plastic wrap and refrigerate for 1 hour.
3. Swordfish
4. Season swordfish steaks on both sides with seasoned salt, to taste.
5. Place on the grill at 400°F for 10 minutes per side. Swordfish is ready when the internal temperature reaches 140°F.
6. Remove the fish and let it rest for 5-10 minutes before serving.
7. Sauce swordfish steaks with lemon-caper sauce and garnish with green onion tops.

Cedar Plank Smoked Salmon

Cooking Time: 1-1.5 Hrs

Ingredients:

- Salmon fillets
- 1/3 C. olive oil
- 1/3 C. soy sauce
- 1/3 C. maple syrup
- ½ Tsp. cayenne pepper

Directions:

1. Rinse salmon and pat dry with paper towel. 2. Mix all ingredients together and pour evenly over salmon in an airtight container. Reserve some for basting and set aside. 3. Place in refrigerator and allow to marinate for 1 hour, or longer if desired. 4. Pre-heat grill to 275°F. Soak cedar planks in water for 3 minutes before placing on the grill to warm for 5-10 minutes. 5. Place salmon on cedar planks and smoke until the internal temperature of the fish reaches 145°F, basting with reserved marinade every 30 minutes.
2. Remove from grill and serve. Enjoy!

Grilled Salmon

Cooking Time: 20 Min

Ingredients:

- 4 Salmon Fillets
- 1/4 Cup of Olive Oil
- 2 Tbsp of Char-Griller Creole Seasoning
- 1/2 Tbsp of Garlic Powder
- 1 Tsp of Dried Parsley
- Kosher Salt
- Ground Black Pepper
- 4 Lemon Wedges

Directions:

1. Generously coat the salmon with olive oil and all seasonings. Heat your grill to medium-high heat. Add salmon fillets, flesh side down, cooking for 6-8 minutes with the grill closed. Once the meat is firm enough, flip it over, closing the lid, cooking for an additional 3-8 minutes depending on desired doneness. Remove from heat and allow the fillets to rest for 5 minutes before removing the skin and serving with lemon wedges along with any desired condiments and toppings.

Grilled Tilapia

Cooking Time: 15-20 Min

Ingredients:

- 3 whole Tilapia
- 2 oz. smoked paprika
- 2 oz. Old Bay seasoning
- Salt and pepper, to taste
- Chopped parsley
- Olive oil
- 4 garlic cloves thinly sliced

Directions:

1. Set up grill for indirect heat and preheat to 350°F.

2. While grill is heating, stuff the inside of each fish with chopped parsley and garlic, then season inside and out with smoked paprika and Old Bay seasoning. Drizzle with olive oil and top with more parsley, smoked paprika/seasoning mix and remaining garlic.

3. Place fish on the grill oiled side down and drizzle with more oil and season with remaining parsley, smoked paprika/seasoning mix. Allow fish to cook for 7-10 minutes on each side.

4. Enjoy!

Grilled Lobster Tails

Cooking Time: 10 Min

Ingredients:

- 8oz. lobster tails
- 2 sticks salted butter
- 1 Tbsp. garlic

Directions:

1. Butterfly the lobster. To do this, use a sharp knife or kitchen shears to split the lobster shell all the way to the tail. Slice the meat in half along the cut line on the shell, being careful not to slice through the lobster. Open the lobster shell-side down and lay it flat. 2. To make clarified butter, melt butter in a pan. Bring to a boil and reduce to a simmer. Skim the foam from the surface. Strain the butter to further remove residue, if desired. Add garlic and stir to combine. Pour into a small bowl and set aside to keep warm. 3. Brush lobster tails with clarified garlic butter and place on the grill, shell-side up, at 400°F for 3-4 minutes. Flip and grill for another 5-6 minutes. Lobster is done when internal temperature reaches 135°F.

Salmon Burger

Cooking Time: 10 Min

Ingredients:

- 10 oz. ground salmon
- 1½ Tbsp. mayonnaise
- 1 Tbsp. Dijon mustard
- 1 Tbsp. horseradish
- 3 scallions, thinly sliced
- ⅛ oz. chives or tarragon, finely chopped
- Juice of 1 lemon
- ¼ C. panko breadcrumbs
- 1 Tbsp. capers, roughly chopped, optional
- Brioche or hamburger buns
- Olive oil
- Salt and pepper, to taste

Directions:

1. Pre-heat grill to 400°F. In a medium bowl, combine salmon, mustard, horseradish, bread crumbs, capers, if using, and scallions. Season with ½ Tsp. salt and pepper, to taste. Mix ingredients by hand until well blended. 2. Form 2 equal patties, about 1" thick. Transfer to a plate and chill in refrigerator until firm, 5-10 minutes. 3. While burgers chill, whisk together mayonnaise, chives (or tarragon, if

substituting), lemon juice, salt and pepper to taste in a small bowl to make aioli. Cover with plastic wrap and refrigerate until ready to serve. 4. Grill salmon burgers for 4-5 minutes on each side, until cooked through and opaque. 5. Place buns cut-side down on grill and toast until lightly browned, 2-3 minutes.

2. To serve spread aioli on salmon burgers and top with condiments of choice. Enjoy!

Creole Blackened Salmon

Cooking Time: 10 Min

Ingredients:

- 1 Salmon Filet
- Avocado Oil
- Char-Griller Creole Seasoning

Directions:

1. Preheat grill to 400F
2. Slice salmon filet into approx 3" portions.
3. Lightly coat portions in avocado oil and season using Creole seasoning.
4. Place salmon on grill (I like to use copper grill mats for fish) grill approx 5-6 minutes, flip salmon and grill another 3-4 minutes.
5. Remove and enjoy!!

Lemon Pepper Shrimp

Cooking Time: 7 Min

Ingredients:

- 1.5 lbs Peel-n-Eat Shrimp
- 1 Tbsp Avocado Oil
- 1/2 Stick Butter, Melted
- 1/2 Tbsp Black Pepper
- 1 Tbsp Lemon Zest
- 1 Tbsp Minced Garlic
- 1 Tbsp Parsley, Chopped
- 1/2 Tbsp Salt

Directions:

1. Fill your chimney with charcoal, and light over side burner flame until coals are lit. Allow them to burn for 20-30 minutes, then release into grill and close lid, allowing grates to heat to high temp.
2. Toss shrimp in avocado oil, and scatter on grill. Close the lid and let shrimp cook 3-5 minutes, until pink and charred. Remove from heat
3. Mix butter with pepper, lemon juice & zest, garlic, salt, and parsley. Toss the hot grilled shrimp in sauce, and serve immediately with tons of napkins! Enjoy!

Rosemary Shrimp Skewers

Cooking Time: 5 Min

Ingredients:

- Shrimp Seasoned with Salt, Pepper, and Jerk Seasoning - 1 Pound
- Fresh Rosemary - Use full stalk and remove half of leaves to expose the stalk, this becomes your skewer

Directions:

1. Skewer two shrimp per skewer
2. Cook on grill at 350 degrees, 5 minutes per side till cooked thoroughly

Grilled Coconut Lime Foil Packets

Cooking Time: 12 To 15 Min

Ingredients:

- 1 Small, Yellow Onion - Chopped
- 3 Garlic Cloves
- Shredded Sweetened Coconut - 1 Cup
- Zest and Juice from 1 Lime

- Fresh Cilantro - 1 Cup
- Extra Virgin Olive Oil - 1/4 Cup
- Soy Sauce - 1/4 Cup
- Raw Shrimp, Peeled and Deveined - 1 Pound
- Corn Kernels - 2 Cups
- 1 Zucchini - Sliced into 1/4 inch rounds and halved
- Halved Cherry Tomatoes - 1 Cup
- Salt and Pepper to Taste
- Fajita Seasoning - 1 tsp

Directions:

1. Using a blender, combine onion, garlic, coconut, lime zest, lime juice, cilantro, olive oil, and soy sauce. Blend until smooth.
2. Place marinade and shrimp in a bowl and toss to coat.
3. Set aside for 5 minutes.
4. Preheat grill to medium high heat.
5. Tear off four large squares of foil.
6. Spray one side of foil with cooking spray.
7. Divide vegetables and shrimp evenly among each packet.
8. Season with salt, pepper and fajita seasoning.
9. Foil up packets and seal completely.
10. Put packets on grill, close the lid, and grill for 6 minutes. Turn packets over and grill for 7 minutes.
11. Open packets and stir.
12. Sprinkle with fresh cilantro and serve.

Shrimp Tacos

Cooking Time: 20 Min

Ingredients:

- 2 Lbs of Shrimp (Tail off, Peeled, and Deveined Shrimp)
- Jalapeno-Lime Seasoning
- Tequila Lime Marinade
- 1 Head Green Cabbage
- 3-4 Jalapenos
- 1 Bundle Cilantro
- White Onion
- Green Onion
- Lime (Zest and Juice)
- Coleslaw Dressing
- 2 Tbsp Sriracha Hot Sauce
- 16 Oz Sour Cream
- Corn Tortillas

Directions:

1. Prep shrimp by removing shell, tail, and devein if this is not already done
2. Season and marinate with Jalapeno-Lime Seasoning and Tequila-Lime Marinade Shred green cabbage and add to large mixing bowl
3. Remove seeds and Julianne jalapenos
4. Chop cilantro and green onions and add to the mixing bowl
5. Add zest and juice from 1 lime
6. Season coleslaw with Jalapeno-Lime seasoning
7. Add coleslaw dressing and mix all together
8. Dice white onion and set aside for taco topping
9. In a separate mixing bowl combine sour cream, Sriracha, Tequila-Lime Marinade, and Jalapeno-Lime seasoning
10. Preheat your grill and cast iron skillet
11. Cook shrimp hot and fast in a cast iron skillet
12. Char tortillas directly on the grill
13. Assemble tacos and enjoy!
14. Pitt Tips: Fresh shrimp is always best, but frozen shrimp works perfectly fine also! NEVER microwave your tortillas!

Blackened Catfish

Cooking Time: 15 Min

Ingredients:

- 4-6 Catfish Filets
- 3-4 Tbsp of Blackening Seasoning (Few Of My Favorites, Mis Rubins Fish Magic, Ashman Bayou Blackening, Pappys Lemon Pepper)
- 2 Tbsp Avocado Oil

Directions:

1. Preheat grill to 450F, I like to use a copper grill mat when grilling fish, works very well. Coat filets with oil and season. Place fish on grill mat, grill 6-8 minutes until you get desired blackened look, flip fish and cook another 3-4 minutes. Remove catfish from grill serve over rice and enjoy!

Spicy Caribbean Shrimp

Cooking Time: 6-8 Min

Ingredients:

- 2 lbs. large shrimp, peeled and deveined
- Pineapple cubes
- 2 C. pineapple juice
- ½ C. coconut milk
- ¼ C. dark rum
- 4 habanero peppers, cored and seeded
- 2 Tsp. lime juice
- Your favorite jerk seasoning, to taste

Directions:

1. Pre-heat grill to 400°F. Combine pineapple juice, coconut milk, dark rum, habanero peppers and lime juice in a blender and mix well. Place shrimp and pineapple cubes on to bamboo skewers and add marinade. Marinate in the refrigerator no longer than 30 minutes in a non-reactive pan, i.e. ceramic or glass. The acid from the lime juice and pineapple juice will cook the shrimp (like in a ceviche) if left in longer. Remove shrimp skewers from marinade and season to taste on both sides with jerk seasoning. Discard marinade. Cook 3-4 minutes per side at 400°F, until shrimp is pink and opaque.

2. Remove from grill and serve!

Seared Sesame Ahi Tuna

Cooking Time: 20 Min

Ingredients:

- 2 Ahi Tuna steaks
- 2 Tbsp. olive oil
- 1 Tsp. sesame oil
- 3 Tbsp. black sesame seeds
- 3 Tbsp. white sesame seeds
- Salt and pepper, to taste
- Wasabi, for serving
- Lemon wedges, for serving
- Soy sauce, for serving

Directions:

1. Pre-heat grill to 400°F. Rinse tuna steaks and pat dry with paper towel. Place steaks on a clean cutting board and coat with olive oil and 1 Tsp. of sesame oil. Season on both sides with salt and pepper, to taste. 2. Toss black and white sesame seeds together in a large bowl and season with salt and pepper, to taste. Press the tuna steaks into the sesame seeds, covering all sides of the steaks. 3. Place the steaks on the grill to sear for 2 minutes on each side, flipping halfway through. Watch the steaks closely so that the sesame seeds don't burn. Use tongs to lift and sear the edges of the steaks. 4. Remove steaks from the grill and allow to rest for 5-10 minutes. Slice the steaks against the grain into 1" thick strips. The steaks should have a rare, bright-red middle.

2. Serve with wasabi, soy sauce and lemon wedges, if desired.

3. Allergy notice: Recipe contains sesame seeds and sesame oil.

Lobster Roll

Cooking Time: 10 Min

Ingredients:

- 8 oz. lobster tails
- ½ C. mayonnaise
- 3 Tbsp. lemon juice
- 2 celery stalks, finely chopped
- 2 Tbsp. fresh parsley leaves, chopped
- 4 rolls, split and lightly toasted
- Melted butter, for brushing
- Salt and pepper, to taste

Directions:

1. Brush lobster with butter and place on the grill, shell-side up, at 400°F for 3-4 minutes. Flip and grill for another 5-6 minutes. Lobster is done when internal temperature reaches 135°F.

2. While lobster is grilling, stir together mayonnaise, lemon juice, celery, parsley in a large bowl and add salt and pepper, to taste.

3. When lobster has cooled, scoop meat from shells and roughly chop. Fold into mayonnaise mixture from Step

4. Butter both sides of rolls and fill with lobster mixture. Enjoy!

Flavor Pro Cedar Plank Salmon

Cooking Time: 25 Min

Ingredients:

- 2 Cedar Planks
- 2 Salmon Filets
- Olive Oil
- Rosemary

- Salt and Pepper to Taste

Directions:

1. Soak cedar planks in water for at least 8 hours. Set up the Flavor Pro for Indirect cooking Add 30 to 40 charcoal briquettes to one side of the flavor drawer Ignite charcoal with gas burners set to medium high Once charcoal is lit, turn off gas burners and allow to fully ash over Rub salmon on both sides with olive oil. Season with salt and pepper, rosemary sprigs and slices of lemon Place Salmon on the side of the grill away from the charcoal Cook salmon for 15 minutes or until flakey.

Honey Sriracha Lime Salmon

Cooking Time: 25 Min

Ingredients:

- 1 Lb Salmon
- 1 Tsp Kosher Salt
- 1/2 Tsp Coarse Black Pepper
- 1/2 Tsp Garlic Powder
- 1 Tsp Olive Oil
- 1/4 Cup Sriracha
- 1/4 Cup Honey
- 2 Garlic Cloves (Minced)
- 1 Lime

Directions:

1. Coat salmon with a light layer of olive oil on both sides. Lightly season with salt, pepper, and garlic powder.

2. Heat grill to 325 F. Place salmon skin side down indirectly from the heat once the grill has reached the targeted temp.

3. In a heat safe bowl combine sriracha, honey, minced garlic, and lime. Bring the mixture to a boil and reduce heat to let simmer. Once salmon has reached an internal temp between 140F -

142F apply a layer of the sauce mixture to the top of the salmon.

4. Once salmon has reached an internal temp of 145 F pull from grill. Garnish with an extra squeeze of lime and cilantro. Serve and enjoy!

Cedar Plank Salmon

Cooking Time: 20-25 Min

Ingredients:

- Whole Coho Salmon 2 Lbs
- Cedar Plank Boards
- Olive Oil
- Kary's Roux All Purpose Seasoning
- Caribeque Lemon Garlic Seasoning
- Lemons
- Dill
- Parsley
- Asparagus (Optional)
- Garlic Parsley Butter

Directions:

1. Soak the cedar plank boards in water for one hour prior to prepping the salmon. Slice the whole salmon into four fillets, it is fine to leave the skin on. Place the salmon fillets on the cedar plank boards with a few lemon slices and asparagus.Tip: Apply olive oil directly on the cedar plank side you place the salmon to keep it from sticking.

2. Apply even coat of olive oil to the top/sides of the salmon fillets. Apply Caribeque Lemon Garlic Seasoning and Kary's Roux All Purpose Seasoning: use to taste. Add Garlic Parsley Butter to the top of each salmon: 1tsp per fillet. Add dill, parsley and additional lemons to the salmon fillets. Sprinkle parsley flakes when done to complete the prepping process.

3. Grilling directions: 20-25 minutes, internal temperature 145°

4. Preheat your grill to 400° Add cedar planks with the salmon to the grill directly over the lump Charcoal. No need to rotate, allow the grill, charcoal and cedar plank salmon to roast the salmon. Tip: It's also okay if your temperature drops: check out the recipe video on YouTube full for temperature control tips. Cook to internal temperature 145° and remove the cedar planks from the

5. Grill and it's ready for immediate eating.Tip: take the guesswork out and use the Char-Griller Grills folding probe to easily see what temperature the salon is at. Enjoy!

Fresh Garlic Parsley Butter Salmon

Cooking Time: 30 Min

Ingredients:

- Garlic Parsley Butter
- 2 (6 oz) Salmon Mignons
- Tajin to Taste
- Dry Parsley Flakes to Taste
- Olive Oil

Directions:

1. Make Garlic Parsley Butter

2. Add Tajin seasoning to butter to taste or use favorite seafood seasoning.

3. Add 1 tbsp. of Fresh Garlic Parsley to each salmon mignons patty.

4. Add dry parsley flakes to taste.

5. Preheat your Char-griller Premium Red Kettle 14822 to 350°.

6. Insert the Char-griller Chimney in the middle of the grill in the fire pit area and do not remove it and no need to release the coals.

7. The handle will not melt inside the Premium Kettles. This will give you a hot fire in the middle of the grill for easy cast iron cooking and also raises the charcoal. The middle small grill grate can be easily moved with a Char-griller grate lifter to add charcoal.

8. Add olive oil to your cast iron skillet: just enough to coat the bottom of the skillet and place over the fire to preheat.

9. Then place the salmon on the cast iron skillet.

10. Flip Salomon after 12 minutes and toss the melted fresh garlic parsley on all sides of the salmon using a spoon.

11. Add 2 additional tbsp. to the skillet for extra flavor.

12. Then move the cast iron skillet away from the middle of the grill for a quick offset cook for 15 minutes.Tip: Continuously add the melted fresh garlic parsley on all sides of the salmon using a spoon for extra flavor.

13. Enjoy!

Spicy Crawfish Dip

Cooking Time: 15 Min

Ingredients:

- ½ C. butter
- ½ C. chopped bell pepper
- ½ C. chopped onion (or green onion)
- 1 Tbsp. basil
- 2 cloves minced garlic
- 2 Tsp. Old bay or Cajun seasoning
- Salt and pepper, to taste
- 1 lb. pack frozen, cooked, peeled crawfish tails, thawed and undrained
- 8 oz. cream cheese, softened
- Sriracha, to taste

Directions:

1. Pre-heat grill to 350°F and add Smokin' Stone under the grates. Place a cast iron skillet on top of the grates and heat until very hot.

2. Add butter to skillet and allow to melt. Add bell pepper and onion. Sauté for 2 minutes, stirring occasionally.

3. Add basil, garlic, seasoning and salt and pepper to taste and stir. Add crawfish and stir to combine.

4. Stir in cream cheese until mixture is smooth. Stir in Sriracha sauce, to taste and allow to smoke for 10 minutes with lid closed at 350°F.

5. Remove from grill and serve with crackers or toasted French bread slices. Enjoy!

Shrimp Po' Boy With Garlic Parsley Butter

Cooking Time: 15 Min

Ingredients:

- 4 cloves chopped fresh garlic
- 1/3 C. chopped fresh parsley
- 1 Tsp. Kosher salt
- 1 stick butter
- 20-25 shrimp, peeled and deveined
- ½ Tbsp. Creole/Cajun seasoning
- 2 Tbsp. Sazón seasoning
- 1 lemon, sliced in half
- 1 Tbsp. chopped fresh parsley (can substitute dried)
- 2-4 cloves chopped fresh garlic
- 3 Tbsp. garlic-parsley butter
- Shredded lettuce
- Tomato slices
- Your favorite bread rolls, sliced lengthwise
- Olive oil for drizzling

Directions:

1. Combine 4 cloves chopped garlic, 1/3 C. chopped parsley, Kosher salt and butter in a medium bowl and mix thoroughly by hand with gloves to make garlic parsley butter.

2. Place bowl in refrigerator to chill and use when needed.

3. Shrimp Po' Boy

4. In a large bowl, season shrimp with Creole/Cajun and Sazón seasonings, or use Original All-Purpose BBQ rub, to taste, and mix well. Add in juice from half lemon, remaining chopped garlic and lightly drizzle with olive oil.

5. Place shrimp in refrigerator for 30 minutes to allow the seasonings to absorb. After 30 minutes, put shrimp on skewers or place in grill wok.

6. Pre-heat grill to 225° and prepare for offset smoking by placing cherry wood chunks or preferred wood chunks in the Side Fire Box. Smoke shrimp for 9 minutes or until the internal temperature reaches 130°F.

7. Char the shrimps over direct heat for 3 minutes on each side or until the internal temperature reaches 140°F. Toast bread rolls until golden brown. Melt garlic parsley butter and toss with shrimp in a bowl until evenly coated.

8. Add shrimp, lettuce and tomatoes to toasted bread rolls and enjoy!

Grilled Seafood Boil

Cooking Time: 20-25 Min

Ingredients:

- 2 Lb. Of Large Shrimp, Deveined and Peeled, Remove the tails during prep if you prefer
- 2 Andouille Sausages (Thinly Sliced)
- 2 Large Ears Of Corn, Shucked and Each Cut Into 4 Small Cobs
- 1 Lb. of Red Bliss potatoes (Cut Into Small Cubes)
- 1 Lemon (Sliced Into 4 Wedges)
- 4 Tbsp of Butter
- 4 Tsp of Char-Griller "Creole" Rub
- 4 Tsp Of Italian Seasoning
- 4 Tsp Of Minced Garlic
- Extra Virgin Olive Oil
- Salt and Pepper To Taste

Directions:

1. Preheat your grill to medium-high heat. Arrange 4 pieces of aluminum foil, about 1 foot long for each packet. Evenly divide shrimp, sausages, corn, potatoes and lemon amongst each "packet". Drizzle each packet with olive oil, 1 tsp of garlic, salt and pepper, and 1 tsp of Char-Griller's Creole seasoning. Use hands to mix to ensure all elements are coated evenly. Top each off packet with 1 tsp of Italian Seasoning, and 1 Tbsp of butter. Fold each packet, ensuring the entire mixture is covered and twist the edges seal it closed. Place the foil packets directly on the grill and cook for 20-25 minutes or until they are cooked to your liking. Serve warm, enjoy!

Steamed Mussels With Pancetta

Cooking Time: 30 Min

Ingredients:

- 2 lbs. fresh mussels, scrubbed and de-bearded
- 4 oz. pancetta, diced
- 3/4 C. dry white wine
- 2 Tbsp. olive oil
- 1/2 onion, diced
- 4 cloves garlic, peeled and minced
- 1 1/4 C. fish stock
- 2 Tbsp. lemon juice
- 2 Tbsp. chives, minced

- 8-10 grape tomatoes, sliced lengthwise
- Pinch of crushed red pepper flakes
- Salt and pepper to taste
- French bread, sliced and toasted for serving

Directions:

1. Add pancetta from Step 1 and mussels to pan and allow to steam with lid closed, until mussels have opened, about 5-10 minutes.

2. Open grill lid and stir in dry white wine, fish stock, lemon juice, chives, sliced tomatoes and crushed red pepper flakes, if desired, and season with salt and pepper, to taste. Simmer for 3-5 minutes until almost all of the liquid is evaporated.

3. Remove pan from the heat and discard any shells that do not open. Serve with toasted French bread. Enjoy!

Shrimp 'n Grits

Cooking Time: 20-25 Min

Ingredients:

- 1 lb. shrimp, peeled and deveined
- Original All-Purpose BBQ rub, to taste, or preferred rub
- ½ red bell pepper, chopped
- ½ onion, chopped
- Handful of cilantro, chopped
- 4 C. water
- 1 Tsp. salt
- 1 C. stone-ground grits
- 2-3 Tbsp. butter
- 4 oz. heavy cream
- 2 oz. Parmesan cheese
- Salt and pepper, to taste

Directions:

1. Pre-heat grill to 375°F. Bring water to a boil, add grits and cook until water is absorbed, about 20- 25 minutes. Remove from heat, stir in butter, cheese and heavy cream. Add salt and pepper, to taste and stir. Set aside. 2. While grits are cooking, melt butter in skillet and sauté red pepper and onions until soft, about 5-7 minutes, stirring occasionally. 3. Add shrimp and season with Original All-Purpose BBQ Rub and cook for 3-5 minutes, until opaque and fully cooked. Add cilantro and salt and pepper, to taste and stir to combine.

2. To serve, spoon grits into bowls and top with shrimp and red pepper mixture. Garnish with more cilantro and enjoy!

Fish Tacos

Cooking Time: 10 Min

Ingredients:

- 1 lb. mahi mahi fillets
- 2 Tbsp. fresh cilantro, finely chopped
- 1 garlic clove, finely chopped
- 2 Tbsp. olive oil
- ¼ head cabbage, thinly sliced
- 2 avocados, peeled, pitted, thinly sliced
- 8 corn tortillas
- 1/3 C. sour cream, for serving
- 1/3 C. fresh cilantro leaves, chopped, for garnish
- Lime wedges, for serving
- Pico de Gallo, for serving
- Salt and pepper, to taste

Directions:

1. Rinse fish and pat dry with paper towel. Place on a platter and season with chopped cilantro, garlic, olive oil and salt and pepper, to taste.

2. Marinate for 30 minutes, or cover and refrigerate to marinate for up to 6 hours.

3. Pre-heat grill to 400°F. Grill fish for 3 minutes per side, until cooked through and

opaque. Turn halfway through for good sear marks. Fish is done when internal temperature reaches 135°F. Remove from grill and allow to rest for 2 minutes.

4. Warm tortillas on the grill until heated through. Remove tortillas from heat and cover to keep warm.

5. Slice the fish into 1" thick strips and divide among tortillas. Top with cabbage, avocado slices, Pico de Gallo, and sour cream. Garnish with cilantro and serve with lime wedges.

Lobster Mac 'n Cheese

Cooking Time: 30-35 Min

Ingredients:

- 8oz. lobster tails
- 1 lb. Cavatappi or elbow macaroni
- 1 qt. milk
- 1 stick unsalted butter, divided
- ½ C. all-purpose flour
- 12 oz. Gruyere cheese, grated
- 8 oz. extra-sharp Cheddar, grated
- 1½ C. breadcrumbs
- ½ Tsp. black pepper
- ½ Tsp. nutmeg
- Kosher salt, to taste

Directions:

1. Butterfly the lobster. To do this, use a sharp knife or kitchen shears to split the lobster shell all the way to the tail. Slice the meat in half along the cut line on the shell, being careful not to slice through the lobster. Open the lobster shell-side down, lay it flat and brush with butter. 2. Place lobster on the grill, meat side down at 375°F for 4-5 minutes. Flip and grill for another 6-7 minutes. 3. While lobster is grilling, make the Mac 'n cheese. Lobster is done when internal

temperature reaches 135°F. 4. Remove lobster from grill and allow to cool. Scoop meat from shells and roughly chop.

2. Mac 'n cheese

3. Pour oil into a large pot of boiling salted water. Add pasta and cook according to package directions, 6-8 minutes. Drain well. 2. Meanwhile, heat the milk in a small saucepan until hot, being careful not to boil it. Whisk together 6 Tbsp. butter and flour in a large pot. Add hot milk and cook for 1-2 minutes, until thickened and smooth. Remove from heat and add cheese, 1 Tbsp. salt, pepper, and nutmeg. Add cooked macaroni and lobster and stir well. Spoon mixture into cast iron pan. 4. Melt the remaining butter, stir in breadcrumbs and sprinkle on top. Place pan on the grill at 375°F and bake for 30- 35 minutes, or until the sauce is bubbly and the macaroni is lightly browned on top.

2-burner Flat Iron Easy Shrimp Tacos

Cooking Time: 10 Min

Ingredients:

- 1 Lb. of medium-sized shrimp, deveined and peeled with tails removed
- 6-8 Flour or Corn Tortillas
- 1 Tbsp of Extra Virgin Olive Oil
- 1 Tbsp of Char-Griller Chili Lime or Taco & Fajita Rub
- 1/2 Tbsp of Garlic Powder
- 1/2 Tbsp of Onion Powder
- 1/2 Tbsp of Pepper
- A Dash of Salt
- Optional Toppings: Iceberg Lettuce, Sour Cream, Tomatoes, Cilantro, Salsa, Avocado

Directions:

1. Make these simple shrimp tacos as complex or as stuffed as you'd like. Our Rubs will take this dish to the next level, preparing it perfectly for whatever your taste buds have in mind.

2. Prep shrimp, by drying as much as possible with paper towels. In a bowl, combine shrimp with olive oil and all seasonings. With Flat Iron preheated to medium-high heat, add shrimp to cooktop and cook while occasionally stirring for about 5-6 minutes or until shrimp are no longer pink. Remove from Flat Iron. Add tortillas to the cooktop and warm up, cooking for 2-3 minutes per side. Assemble the tacos with desired toppings and serve immediately. Enjoy!

Seared Scallops With Pancetta

Cooking Time: 15 Min

Ingredients:

- 12 U-10 Scallops
- 4 oz. pancetta, chopped
- ½ red onion or 1 shallot, minced
- 2 C. green peas, drained and divided
- 4 oz. Parmesan cheese
- 1 Tbsp. olive oil
- Juice of 1 lemon
- 4 oz. mint, divided
- Salt and pepper, to taste

Directions:

1. Pre-heat grill to 375°F. Fry pancetta in a cast iron pan for about 5 minutes and drain grease. Add minced red onion (or shallot, if substituting) and 1 C. peas to pan and season with salt and pepper, then add ½ of mint and stir to incorporate. Cook until warmed through. 2. Combine 1 C. peas and lemon juice, remaining mint, olive oil and Parmesan cheese in a food processor. Season to taste with salt and pepper and blend until smooth. 3. Rinse scallops and pat dry with paper towel. Season scallops with salt and pepper to taste on all sides. Place on the grill and sear for 3-5 minutes per side.

2. To serve, spoon peas onto plate, add scallops and top with pancetta mixture. Enjoy!

Oysters "dougie-feller"

Cooking Time: 15 Min

Ingredients:

- 10-12 Large Oysters
- 2 oz. pancetta
- 2-3 Tbsp. shallot, chopped
- 2 Tbsp. unsalted butter
- 4 cloves minced garlic
- 3 Tbsp. hot pepper sauce
- 2 oz. panko crumbs
- Juice of ½ lemon
- 2 C. spinach, chopped
- Bed of rock salt

Directions:

1. Shuck oysters

2. Melt 2 Tbsp. unsalted butter in cast iron skillet

3. Sauté pancetta in skillet until crispy (5-7 minutes)

4. Add chopped shallot, and cook until fragrant, about 1 minute

5. Add 4 cloves minced garlic, cook until fragrant, about 1 minute

6. Add 3 Tbsp. hot pepper sauce, stir to incorporate

7. Mix in chopped spinach

8. Sauté until spinach begins to wilt

9. Add 2 oz of panko crumbs

10. Season with salt and pepper to taste

11. Stir in lemon juice

12. Remove from heat and set aside

13. Place 10-12 large oysters on grill at 350°F, shell side up, cooking for 5-7 minutes

14. Remove from grill and lay oysters on a bed of rock salt

15. Top oysters with pancetta and spinach mixture

Fish And Chips

Cooking Time: 12 Min

Ingredients:

- 4 cod filets
- 3-4 Idaho potatoes
- 1 C. flour
- 1 C. milk
- 1 egg
- 1 Tsp. Old Bay seasoning

Directions:

1. Heat grill to 350-400°F.

2. Let oil heat up in skillet until it sizzles when splashed with a few drops of water.

3. 3-4 Idaho potatoes with skin on, cut into french fries.

4. Let them soak in water for 20-30 minutes to remove excess starch.

5. Pat dry on paper towels before frying.

6. Fries are done when they begin to turn golden

7. Mix batter until only a few clumps of flour remain. Don't over mix.

8. Dredge fish in flour seasoned in Old Bay, if you prefer, before dipping in batter

9. Let fish filets fry on each side for 2-3 minutes, until golden crispy brown.

10. Serve with coleslaw and tartar sauce. Delicious!

Grilled Chilean Sea Bass

Cooking Time: 30 Min

Ingredients:

- Whole Chilean Sea bass
- 2 oz. parsley, chopped
- 1½ oz. Original All-Purpose BBQ Rub or your favorite seafood seasoning
- 2 lemons, sliced
- 2-3 sprigs of dill
- Salt and pepper, to taste
- 4 oz. olive oil

Directions:

1. Pre-heat grill to 350°F. Place the charcoal on one side for indirect heat.

2. Score fish diagonally on each side in the thickest part of the meat.

3. Stuff the inside cavity with dill sprigs and lemon slices.

4. Season both sides of the outside of the fish to taste with olive oil, salt and pepper and top with an even layer of Original All-Purpose BBQ Rub, or use your favorite seafood seasoning, and parsley.

5. Lay the fish on the grill for 5-7 minutes on direct heat, then move to the indirect heat side for 15-20 minutes.

BEEF

Arrachera Skirt Steak Tacos

Cooking Time: 10-12 Min

Ingredients:

- 3 lb. Arrachera/Skirt Steak
- Sazón seasoning, three packets or to taste
- Adobo seasoning, to taste
- Meat seasoning, to taste
- 32 oz. bottle of Tecate or your favorite Mexican beer
- 8 limes (6 for the brine, 1 for the avocado dip, 1 for the tacos)
- 1 bunch green onions, ends removed
- 1 jalapeño, seeded, cored and sliced
- 1 onion, diced
- 1 bunch cilantro, chopped
- Corn or Flour tortillas
- Olive Oil

Directions:

1. Pour 32oz of Tecate or your favorite Mexican beer into a large resealable plastic bag and add the juice from 6 limes. Measure out and add the Sazón, Adobo and meat seasonings, to taste.
2. Tip: Add the squeezed lime peels to the bag for additional flavor and also to squeeze on the steak while it's cooking.
3. Mix brine thoroughly and add the steak, green onions and sliced jalapeño and gently shake to evenly coat. Marinate in the refrigerator for 2 hours or best overnight.
4. Arrachera/Skirt Steak
5. Pre-heat the grill to as hot as you can get it.
6. Tip: Spray grill grates with canned olive or vegetable oil.

7. Add green onions and jalapeño and grill until charred or to personal preference. Add steak to the grill for 5-6 minutes on each side or to personal preference.
8. Tip: Squeeze lime peels on to the steak while it's cooking. The limes become filled with the beer brine and the additional flavor and moisture it adds is amazing.
9. Tip: Also add additional meat seasoning to both sides of the steak while on the grill.
10. Remove the steak from the grill and allow it to rest for 5-10 minutes before slicing. Warm tortillas on the grill for about 1 minute.
11. Tip: Brush both sides of each tortilla lightly with olive oil.
12. Gather the onions, cilantro and avocado dip and create your tacos. Serve with salsa, limes, green onions, jalapeño and tortilla chips.
13. Enjoy!

Bbq Fiends Barbacoa Tacos

Cooking Time: 5 Hrs

Ingredients:

- Beef Cheeks - 2 to 3 lbs
- Kosher Salt - 1 Tbsp
- Coarse Black Pepper - 1 Tbsp
- Olive Oil - 1 tsp
- Beef Broth (Low Sodium) - 2 Cups
- 1 White Onion
- Tortillas - 12
- Cilantro (optional)

Directions:

1. Combine salt and pepper in a shaker for easy application. Unwrap beef cheeks and trim excess fat and silver skin off the meat.

2. Rub down the meat with olive oil for a binder and season evenly with your salt/pepper mixture.

3. Start working on getting the fire going and your smoker up to 275 F. Once your smoker is at 275 F you can add a water pan to the side of your grill that is closest to the fire. This will help with keeping your beef cheeks moist. Center the beef cheeks on the middle of the grill and let the smoker do the work.

4. Once the beef cheeks have reached around 165 F internal temp it is time to braise (this should be around the 3-hour mark).

5. Apply a layer of onion slices to the bottom of an aluminum pan. Set your beef cheeks on top of the layer of onions.

6. Carefully pour the beef broth into the pan and make sure to cover the pan completely with aluminum foil.

7. Put the pan back into the smoker and continue to maintain a temperature of 275 F.

8. Once the beef cheeks have reached an internal temp between 203-205 F it is time to take them off the smoker and let rest for 10 minutes. The beef cheeks should be very tender and falling apart when probed.

9. After the beef cheeks have rested for 10 minutes inside of the pan it is time to remove them from the pan and shred them on a cutting board.

10. Once your barbacoa is all shredded go ahead and fill your tortillas with the delicious meat and serve with diced onions and cilantro!

11. Enjoy your barbacoa tacos with your family and friends!

Smoked Beef Ribs

Cooking Time: 7-10 Hrs

Ingredients:
- 1 4-5 lb. Rack Of Beef Ribs
- Water and Apple Cider Vinegar in a spray bottle
- 2 Tbsp of Kosher Salt
- 2 Tbsp of Ground Black Pepper
- 1 Tsp of Brown Sugar
- 1 Tsp of Brown Sugar
- 1 Tsp of Brown Sugar
- 1 Tsp of Cayenne Pepper

Directions:
1. Alternatively, you can use your favorite pre-mixed rub/seasoning.

2. Preheat your smoker to 225-250°F. Thoroughly mix the rub ingredients together. Ensure your ribs are as dry as possible for the crispiest exterior. Pat dry with paper towels if necessary. Coat the exterior of your ribs in the rub mix, massaging it with hands to make sure it is thoroughly rubbed into the meat. Place the ribs into the smoker, fat side up with a water pan underneath close to the Side Fire Box. Close the lids and allow to smoke for 2-3 hours before beginning to spritz with water/vinegar mixture every hour until internal temperature reaches 200-203°F. This process should be 7-10 hours depending on the rack. Remove the ribs from the smoker and wrap in butcher paper, allowing them to rest for an hour before slicing and serving.

Beer Brined Grilled Costillas Beef Short Ribs

Ingredients:
- 2 lbs of Costillas/Beef Short Ribs
- Chef Merito Carne/Meat Seasoning: to taste.
- 32 oz Tecate Beer or favorite Mexican beer.
- 6 Limes.

- One Jalapeño (Sliced)
- One Serrano (Sliced)
- Four Cebollitas
- Olive Oil: Light Drizzle
- Char-Griller Grills Akorn Kamado, Blue
- Fogo Quebracho Lump Charcoal.

Directions:

1. Use a large plastic zip bag or bowl. Slice & squeeze limes. Add beer. Tip: add the squeezed lime peels to the zip baggie or bowl for additional flavor and also to squeeze on the Costillas/Beef Short Ribs when grilling. Add Chef Merito Carne/Meat Seasoning to taste Slice & Add Jalapeno Slice & Add Serrano Mix beer brine thoroughly. Add Cebollitas Once the brine is mixed, add it to the Costillas/Beef Short Ribs & sliced Jalapeño. Then rest for a minimum of two hours. Best if it rests for 24 hours.

2. Grilling/Cooking

3. Pre-heat grill to 370°-400° Tip: spray grill grates with canned Olive, canola or Vegetable oil. Add cebollitas, limes & jalapeño to the grill. Add the Costillas/Beef Short Ribs to the grill. Grill for 8-10 minutes on each side or to personal preference. Tip: squeeze lime peels on to the meat while it's cooking. The limes become filled with the beer brine and the additional flavor and moisture it adds is amazing. Tip: also add additional Chef Merito Carne/Meat Seasoning to both sides of the meat while on the grill. When the meat is removed. Allow it to rest for 5-10 minutes before slicing/dicing. After resting slice and dice the meat Warm tortillas on grill for roughly one minute. Tip: lightly and olive oil to both sides of the tortillas. Serve with fresh salsa, limes, jalapeño & tortilla chips. Enjoy

Flat Iron Griddle Beef Shank Quesadilla Tacos With Consumé

Cooking Time: 5:10 Hrs

Ingredients:

- 1-2 Pounds of Beef Shank
- Small Bundle Of Cilantro (Chopped or Whole)
- 1 Onion (Diced)
- 3 Garlic Cloves
- 1 Cup Chihuahua Cheese
- Sazón, Adobo & Char Griller Grills Taco Fajita Seasonings (Use Seasonings To Taste.)
- Beef Stock 32 Oz
- 1 Pack Of Corn Tortillas
- 1-2 Limes (Cut Into Quarters)
- Char-Griller Flat Iron Griddle

Directions:

1. Instruction

2. Beef Shank Cooking Directions

3. Seasoned the beef shank meat with Sazón, Adobo & Char Griller Grills Taco Fajita seasonings to taste with ½ onion and three garlic cloves. On stove or Char-Griller Grills side burner on low boil the beef shank in the beef stock for roughly five hours or until it's soft and tender. Shred the beef. Strain the beef juice for the consomé that is used for dipping. Added a bit of water and additional Sazón, Adobo & Char Griller Grills Taco Fajita seasonings and simmered for few minutes. Now it's time to fire up the Flat Iron Griddle for the beef shank quesadilla tacos with consumé.

4. Flat Iron Griddle Beef Shank Quesadilla Tacos with consume Cooking Directions

5. Fire up your Flat Iron Griddle to medium heat. Have the beef shank meat and consume on

top of the griddle off to the side. ⊠ Add cheese and then the shredded beef shank to the hot griddle top and also the tortillas. Once the cheese melts, add one tortilla on top of the shredded beef and then flip. After flipping it, add another tortilla to the top of the melted cheese and then add a ladle full of the consumé and cook for an additional few minutes. Repeat this process until all your Beef Shank Quesadilla Tacos completed. Added fresh chopped onions, limes and cilantro to the consumé. Dip the Beef Shank Quesadilla Tacos in the consumé and enjoy!

Biscuits, Briskets, And Gravy

Cooking Time: 30 Min

Ingredients:
- 1 Cup Chopped Brisket
- 1 Package Of Biscuits (6-8 Count)
- 3 1/2 Tbsp Unsalted Butter
- 3 Tbsp All-Purpose Flour
- 2 Cups Whole Milk
- 1 Tsp Kosher Salt
- 1 Tsp Coarse Black Pepper

Directions:
1. Preheat grill to 325 F. Place biscuits on a wire rack and cook indirectly from heat source.
2. Place a medium size pan over the heat source and add butter, stirring until melted. Add flour and stir until it is well mixed with the melted butter. Add the milk and continue to stir until the mixture is well blended and starting to bubble.
3. Once the gravy has a thick consistency add the brisket, salt, and pepper. Stir until well blended and bubbling.
4. Remove the gravy from the heat and pour onto the biscuits. Serve and enjoy!

Flat Iron Steak Fajitas

Cooking Time: 20 Min

Ingredients:
- 2 lb. flat iron steaks
- 1 C. soy sauce
- 1½ C. pineapple juice
- 1 Tbsp. ground cumin
- 1½ Tsp. fresh garlic, minced
- 3 Tbsp. fresh squeezed lime juice
- 1 Tsp. Original All-Purpose BBQ rub
- 1 Tsp. olive oil
- 1 yellow onion, sliced lengthwise
- 1-2 bell peppers, seeded and sliced lengthwise
- 6" flour tortillas
- Cilantro, chopped, for garnish
- Shredded cheese (optional)
- Pico de Gallo and/or guacamole, for serving

Directions:
1. Whisk soy sauce, pineapple juice, cumin, garlic and lime juice together in a large bowl to make marinade. Transfer to a large resealable plastic bag with flat iron steaks and gently shake to evenly coat. Marinate in refrigerator for 4 hours or best overnight. 2. Pre-heat grill to 400°F. Heat olive oil in a large sauté pan over high heat. Add onions to pan and cook for 2-3 minutes, stirring constantly. Add peppers to pan and sauté for 3-4 minutes. Season with 1 Tsp. of Original All-Purpose BBQ rub or your favorite rub. Remove pan from heat. 3. Place steaks on grill for 5-7 minutes per side for medium rare. Steak is done when internal temperature reaches 140°F.
2. Slice steak across the grain. Place vegetables on a heated cast iron fajita platter. Place sliced Flat Iron steaks on top of the vegetables. Serve with tortillas, Pico de Gallo, cilantro and guacamole. Top with shredded cheese, if desired.

Chili In A Bread Bowl

Ingredients:

- 2 Lbs Ground Beef
- 8 Hot Link Sausages
- 8 Hot Italian Sausage
- 5 McCormick Mild Chili Seasoning Packets
- 2 Red Onions
- 1 Red Bell Pepper
- 1 Green Bell Pepper
- 2 Jalapenos
- 4 Garlic Cloves
- 4 10oz Cans of Diced Tomatoes and Green Chilies
- 2 Cans Pinto Beans
- 2 Cans Red Kidney Beans
- Shredded Cheese
- Bread Loaf (Bread Bowls)

Directions:

1. Chop your green pepper, red pepper, and red onion Using the Side Burner on our Triple Play, cook ground beef with diced garlic and jalapenos in a large pot Once the beef is cooked, add the 4 cans of diced tomatoes and green chilies Add the 4 cans of beans and mix to combine Add the 5 McCormick seasoning packets Now that your sausages are charred, slice them all and add to the pot Simmer for 30-45 minutes Hollow out your bread loaf with a paring knife to create the bowls Serve in the bread bowls and top with shredded cheese and raw red onions (or whatever else you like!)

2. Pitt Tips: Spice it up a little more by adding your favorite hot sauce, we like Tapatio! Add even more flavor by adding in your favorite beer!

Smoked Corned Beef

Ingredients:

- 3-5 Lb Corned Beef Brisket
- 1 Tbsp of Onion Powder
- 1 Tbsp of Garlic Powder
- 2 Tbsp of Paprika
- 2 Tbsp of Coriander Powder
- 2 Tbsp of Black Pepper
- 3 Tbsp of Brown Sugar

Directions:

1. Place corned beef brisket in a bowl covered with water. Refrigerate overnight, Preheat the smoker between 250-275 degrees by adding desired coals and/or wood to the Side Fire Box. If you do not own a Side Fire Box, no problem! To accomplish the same effect, simply arrange coals and/or wood opposite your cooking area. If you want to place your brisket on the right side of the grates, then arrange coals/wood on the left side, etc. Add desired wood chips to the smoker. Combine seasonings and spices in a bowl to create rub Remove the meat from the water and use paper towels to pat dry. Prepare meat by trimming excess fat if you desire. Coat the meat all over with the rub. Place meat in the smoker until the internal temperature reaches 160 degrees.(2-3 hours) Wrap the meat in butcher paper or aluminum foil and return to the smoker until the internal temperature reaches 195 degrees. (2-3 hours) Allow the meat the rest for a minimum of 30 minutes before slicing Serve warm, enjoy!

Beef Brisket

Cooking Time: 12 Hrs

Ingredients:

- 10 lb. beef brisket
- Rosemary salt, to taste
- Coarse ground pepper

Directions:

1. Place 1 C. packed fresh rosemary leaves and 1 C. coarse salt in a food processor and pulse until the texture resembles table salt. 2. Transfer to a large bowl and add 1 C. Kosher or sea salt and mix well. 3. Spread evenly on a baking sheet to dry for 1-2 hours, then pour into a jar with an airtight lid. Keeps indefinitely.

2. Beef brisket

3. Pre-heat grill to 275°F. Using a sharp knife, trim the fat from the brisket leaving an even, thin layer on the top. 2. Season brisket generously on both sides with rosemary salt, coarse black pepper and your favorite dry rub, or use Original All-Purpose BBQ rub, to taste. Place brisket on the grill fat side up, with a Smokin' Stone or heat deflector under the grates, and allow brisket to smoke at 275°F for 12 hours or until internal temperature reaches 190°F.

4. Let rest for 5-10 minutes before slicing and serving.

Smoked Beef Chili

Cooking Time: 4 Hrs

Ingredients:

- Chuck Roast - 2 Lbs
- 1 Tbsp Kosher Salt (for beef)
- 1 Tbsp Coarse Black Pepper (for beef)
- 1 tsp Garlic Powder (for beef)
- 1 Tbsp Olive Oil (for beef)
- 3 Tbsp Vegetable Oil
- 1 Large Yellow Onion (Diced)
- 6 Garlic Cloves (Minced)
- 1/4 Cup Chili Powder
- 1 Tbsp Ground Cumin
- 1 (28 oz) Can Diced Tomatoes
- 1 (14 oz) Can Tomato Sauce
- 2 (15 oz) Cans Red Kidney Beans (Rinsed)
- Salt and Pepper to Taste
- Fritos, Cheddar Cheese, Cilantro (Toppings)

Directions:

1. Heat your Char-Griller to a temperature of 275 F. Rub the chuck roast with olive oil and season with the mixture of salt, pepper, and garlic powder. Place chuck roast in the Char-Griller away from the fire.

2. When the chuck roast has reached an internal temp of 165 F pull from the grill and let rest. After 10 minutes cut the chuck roast into cubes.

3. Heat the vegetable oil in a large pan and add onions, season with salt/pepper to taste. Cook until onions have softened.

4. Add minced garlic, chili powder, and cumin to the onions and stir until fragrant. Add the cubed chuck roast and stir until coated with the chili mixture.

5. Transfer the chili mixture into a Dutch oven and add the diced tomatoes, tomato sauce, and beans. Stir well to combine.

6. Place Dutch oven back on grill and continue to cook at a temperature of 275 F. Stir occasionally.

7. When chili has melded, and the beef is fork tender it is ready to serve. Serve with your favorite chili toppers and enjoy!

All American Blended Burger

Cooking Time: 15 Min

Ingredients:

- 80/20 Ground Chuck - 3 Ounces
- Baby Portabella Mushrooms - 1 Ounce
- Tomato - 1
- Green Leaf Lettuce - 1 Head
- Ketchup - 1 Tablespoon
- Mayonnaise - 1 Tablespoon
- Char-Griller Steak Rub - 2 Tablespoons
- Brioche Bun

Directions:

1. Chop mushrooms into pieces roughly the size of the grind of the beef.
2. Mix mushrooms and beef together and form a patty.
3. Bring your AKORN up to roughly 600 degrees.
4. Place the burger patty on the grill and season top side with 1 Tbsp of Char-Griller steak rub and let cook for four minutes.
5. Flip the burger, season the now top side with 1 Tbsp of Char-Griller steak rub, continue cooking until an internal temp of 140 degrees is reached.
6. Remove the burger from the grill to let rest. While resting place your bun on the grill to toast. After toasting apply mayo to the bottom bun and ketchup to the top.
7. Add cheese to the burger if desired and build burger from the bottom up as bun, burger, tomato slice, green leaf lettuce top bun and enjoy.

Chi-lanta Pork Belly Burnt Ends

Cooking Time: 4.45 Hrs

Ingredients:

- Pork Belly
- Sharp Knife
- Olive Oil
- Blues Hog Original BBQ Sauce
- Sweet Baby Rays Barbecue Sauce
- Char-Griller Grills Rib Rub
- Foil
- Butter (Not Margarine)
- Apple Juice (Non From Concentrate)
- Pan
- Drip Pan
- Baking Rack
- Golden Protective Services Nitrile Powder Free Gloves For Food Safety

Directions:

1. Prepping: Using a sharp knife slice and remove the skin and excess fat from the pork belly.
2. Slice into cubes
3. Coat with olive oil
4. Season with Char-Griller Rib Rub
5. Smoking
6. Fire up your Char-Griller Grill to 250°.
7. Place drip pan filled with water under the grill grates.
8. Place the pork belly on the baking rack.
9. Spritz every 30 minutes with Apple Juice and rotate the baking rack for even smoking.
10. After 3 hours of smoking, remove the pork belly from the baking rack and place directly in a pan with Apple Juice, Char-Griller Rib Rub, Butter & cover the pan with foil.
11. Place covered pan into the Smoker/Grill and cook for an additional 90 minutes.
12. Remove foil and discard the juices and then add BBQ sauce to the pork belly and mix.
13. Smoke uncovered for an additional 15 minutes and are done.
14. Enjoy.

Oktoberfest Beef Short Ribs

Cooking Time: 3.5 Hrs

Ingredients:

- 6 Lbs Beef Short Ribs
- 1 Package Brown Gravy Mix
- 1 Cup Beef Broth
- 1/8 Cup Beef Seasoning of Choice
- 3 Tbs Brown Sugar
- 3 Tbs Worcestershire Sauce
- 1 Package Egg Noodles

Directions:

1. While these short ribs are definitely going to get their time in the smoke, they aren't exactly your traditional take on beef BBQ, but on cooler days this is going to hit the spot.

2. Serving these ribs up with a gravy over noodles much like beef stroganoff is a really fun way to take what you've learned about smoking meats, applying that knowledge to another dish, and really pushing it over the top with it. Char-Griller Ambassador Steve Dotson of Cookout Coach had a lot of fun making these and he hopes you will too.

3. Load Char-Griller AKORN with charcoal and light ¾ chimney full of charcoal. Once the chimney is completely lit add it to the AKORN along with one chunk of hickory wood.

4. Place the Cooking Stone in place along with the grate and allow the AKORN to come up to 300 degrees with no or light visible smoke.

5. Trim the fat cap off of 6 pounds of beef short ribs and cut into individual ribs..

6. Season with your preferred beef seasonings and rubs.

7. Place ribs on the smoker and let them smoke for two hours.

8. At the two hour mark combine all sauce ingredients into a half sized foil pan and place ribs in the sauce, cover ribs with thinly sliced half of a sweet onion and cover with foil.

9. Place covered pan back on the cooker for another hour and a half.

10. Check for probe tenderness and an internal temp of roughly 210 degrees. If the ribs are tender let them rest for a minimum of half an hour.

11. Prepare egg noodles according to package directions.

12. Remove short ribs from the bone and serve over noodles with sauce ladled over the top.

Italian-style Meatballs

Cooking Time: 10 Min

Ingredients:

- 1 lb. ground chuck
- ½ lb. ground pork
- ¾ C. breadcrumbs
- 2 eggs, lightly beaten
- 1/3 C. grated Parmesan
- 1/3 C. grated Pecorino Romano
- 2 cloves garlic, minced
- 2 Tbsp. finely chopped fresh parsley
- ¼ Tsp. red pepper flakes, optional
- Olive oil, for brushing
- Salt and pepper, to taste
- Marinara sauce, for serving
- Slider buns, for serving, optional

Directions:

1. Pre-heat grill to 400°F. Combine chuck, pork, breadcrumbs, eggs, Parmesan and Pecorino cheeses, garlic, parsley, and red pepper flakes in a large bowl and mix by hand until just blended. 2. Roll mixture into 1½" diameter meatballs. Season

generously with salt and pepper, to taste. 3. Brush meatballs with olive oil and place on grill. Turn occasionally until well-browned on all sides and cooked through, 2-3 minutes per side. 4. Remove meatballs, serve with your favorite sauce and top with more cheese, if desired.

2. Alternately, transfer grilled meatballs and sauce to a pan on medium heat and turn to evenly coat. Serve on toasted slider buns, if desired.

Crab-stuffed Grilled Flank Steak With Asparagus

Cooking Time: 30 Min

Ingredients:
- 2 lb. flank steak
- 6-8 oz. crab meat
- 4 oz. cream cheese, softened
- 1 bunch asparagus, divided
- ¼ C. parsley, chopped
- 2 Tsp. garlic powder
- 2 Tbsp. olive oil
- 2 Tsp. salt, or to taste
- 2 Tsp. pepper, or to taste

Directions:
1. Flank Steak:Remove any excess fat and sinew from the flank steak. Rinse steak and pat dry with paper towel. 2. Butterfly the flank steak lengthwise, keeping the knife parallel and stopping approximately ½ inch from the other long edge, until the meat can open like a book. 3. Generously season flank steak with salt, pepper and garlic powder. 4. Spread an even layer of cream cheese on the steak. 5. Sprinkle parsley evenly on top of the cream cheese layer. 6. Spread crab meat evenly on top of cream cheese/parsley layer.. 7. Starting at one end, roll steak and fillings tightly, and tie securely in multiple spots

with kitchen twine. Snip off any excess twine. 8. Brush steak roll with olive oil, salt and pepper, flipping over to evenly coat top and bottom. 9. Place steak on direct heat at 400°F and sear for 2 minutes on each side, rotating a quarter turn each time. 10. Transfer steak to indirect heat side of grill and cook 20-25 minutes until internal temperature reaches 140-145°F. 1 Remove from the grill, allow to rest for 8-10 minutes before slicing in 1"-1½" increments. 12. Cut and remove kitchen twine before serving.

2. Asparagus:

3. Rinse asparagus spears and cut off the ends.

4. Coat lightly with olive oil and season with salt and pepper, to taste.

5. Place asparagus on the grill at 400°F and cook for 4-5 minutes.

Weeknight Smokehouse Ribs

Cooking Time: 75 Min

Ingredients:
- 2.5 Lbs Baby Back Rib
- 1/2 Cup Char-Griller Ribs Rub
- 1 Cup BBQ Sauce

Directions:
1. Clean ribs and remove silver skin membrane from the back of the ribs. If you're unsure how, slide a butter knife in-between the thick membrane and the meat, and slide until a pocket forms, allowing you to grab and easily peel away. Generously coat the ribs in the rub, and rub in, letting the ribs absorb all of the seasoning.

2. In the instant pot, add 1 cup of water, and the steaming tray to the bottom of the pot. Arrange your ribs, in a coil type shape on their side, and close lid- setting to seal. Select "Pressure Cook",

high pressure, for 28 minutes. Let the IP do its thing.

3. Next, in your Char-Griller Charcoal Chimney, all charcoal, and alternating layers of hickory chunks. Place over burner on the Texas Trio, and light- letting the flame stay burning for about 2-3 minutes, until charcoal lights and begins to burn on it's on. Kill the heat and allow the charcoal to heat up for 20 minutes.

4. Next, add charcoal and wood to the smoking box on the Trio, and add 1-2 more large pieces of wood. Secure your air vents for a slow, steady inflow of air, and prepare your grates.

5. Once the instant pot is done cooking, manual release the steam, and remove ribs. Transfer to the Trio, and close the lid for 20 minutes, allowing the smoke to wrap around the ribs. 20 minutes later, slather the ribs in sauce, and close lid again, until sauce changes from a bright color, to a more sticky, darker hue, about 15 more minutes. Ribs are ready to serve! Enjoy!

Skirt Steak Pinwheels

Cooking Time: 10 Min

Ingredients:

- Skirt Steak- 1 Pound
- Chopped Chives- 1/4 Cup
- Diced Fresh Tomato- 1/4 Cup
- Minced Garlic- 1 Tablespoon
- Salted Butter- 1 Stick
- J Christopher Co. The Rub- 1 Tablespoon
- Vegetable Oil- 1 Teaspoon
- Wooden Skewers- 2

Directions:

1. 30 minutes before prep: Soak wooden skewers in water to avoid burning.

2. Prepare your Akorn or your favorite Char-Griller grill for direct high heat.

3. Lay out skirt steak and slice long way down the middle to make two evenly wide pieces. Each piece should be about 2 inches wide. Lay pieces out flat.

4. Prepare butter. In small mixing bowl add butter, vegetable oil, minced garlic, and The Rub. With spoon, mash butter until your able to whip smooth.

5. Spread butter mixture on the two skirt steak pieces. Sprinkle on chives and tomatoes.

6. Start at end closest to you and roll steak up and away from you, pulling in as you go to keep pinwheel tight. Once rolled, slide wooden skewer through the steak as if you were making a beef lollipop.

7. Sprinkle both sides of the pinwheels with The Rub and place directly on the grill over direct high heat. Shut lid and let cook 5 minutes, turn, and cook another 3-5 minutes with lid closed. Both sides should be seared and brown. I find cooking these to a medium warm pink center rather than medium rare allows for a more tender bite with this cut.

8. Let rest 5-10 minutes and enjoy!

Ultimate Stack Burger

Cooking Time: 16 Min

Ingredients:

- 2 lbs. ground beef
- ¼ lb. bacon
- 4 slices Extra Sharp Cheddar
- 4 slices Swiss cheese
- 1 red onion, sliced
- 1 tomato, sliced
- 4 lettuce leaves

- 1-2 Tsp. Worcestershire sauce
- 1-2 Tbsp. Steak BBQ rub
- Hamburger dill pickle slices, optional
- 4 hamburger buns
- Condiments of choice

Directions:

1. Place ground beef in large bowl and season with Steak BBQ rub, or your favorite rub and Worcestershire sauce. Mix all ingredients by hand until just blended. 2. Form 1" thick patties and place on a wax paper lined tray. Place tray with patties in refrigerator and allow to chill for 10-15 minutes. 3. Fry bacon in batches, if needed, in a pan to desired crispness according to package directions, drain grease and set aside. 4. Place burgers from tray directly on the grill at 400°F for 8 minutes per side, with a quarter turn halfway through for good sear marks. 5. Flip burgers after 8 minutes, add bacon and top with cheese. 6. Allow cheese to melt. Burgers are done when internal temperature reaches 165°F. 7. Let burgers rest for 3-5 minutes before building the burger.

London Broil N' Veggie Skewers

Ingredients:
- 2 Pounds London Broil cut into cubes.
- 2 Ounces of Char-Griller Steak
- 1 Ounce Soy Sauce
- 2 Ounces of Honey Mustard.
- 2 Ounces of White Wine Vinegar.
- 2/3 Cup of Extra Virgin Olive Oil
- 1 Ounce Sazón
- 1 Ounce of Fresh Cilantro (Chopped)
- 1 White Onion (Cut into Squares)
- 1 Yellow Pepper (Cut Into Squares)
- 12-15 Baby Bella Mushrooms (Remove Stem)
- 1 Red Pepper (Cut Into Squares)

Directions:

1. Marinade prep.
2. Using a large bowl mix olive oil, cilantro, sazón, steak rub, white wine vinegar, honey mustard & soy sauce. Mix thoroughly.
3. Then add the London Broil meat to the mixture. Mix thoroughly.
4. Allow to rest for 2-24 hours.
5. Skewer prep
6. Add veggies and meat to long metal or bamboo skewers.
7. Tip: I used long metal skewers, the metal skewers helps cook the meat inside quicker due to the heat transferring from the metal. Bamboo skewers are always a good option but tend to burn on the tips and you also have to remember to soak them prior to prepping/cooking them.
8. Preheat your smoker/grill to 340°-350°: allow the grill/smoker to thoroughly warm.
9. Add skewers to the grill and cook for 15 minutes: turn skewers periodically.
10. baste with warmed mixture of olive oil, cilantro, sazón, steak rub, white wine vinegar, honey mustard & soy sauce.
11. Remove after 15 minutes or desired internal temperature and enjoy.

Pork Brisket Burnt Ends

Ingredients:
- 2 Lbs Pork Brisket
- 4 Tbsp Blues Hog Original Rub
- 1/4 C Blues Hog Pork Marinade
- 1 Cup of Water
- 1/2 Cup Blues Hog Smokey Mountain Sauce

Directions:

1. Preheat grill to 300F and setup for indirect cooking. Trim silver skin and fat from top of pork brisket. Mix water and pork marinade in bowl and place trimmed brisket in marinade, marinate for 1 hr. Remove pork brisket from marinade and season using Blues Hog Original rub. Smoke pork brisket until internal temp reaches 190F, remove from heat, cut brisket into cubes and place in foil pan, sprinkle more Rub on top and add sauce. Place back on grill for 30 minutes, remove, serve and enjoy!

Smoked Prime Rib

Cooking Time: 8 Hrs

Ingredients:

- 15 lb. Prime Rib
- 2 oz. ground pepper
- 4 oz. coarse salt
- 2 oz. smoked paprika

Directions:

1. Mix salt, pepper, and paprika.
2. Cover rib side of prime rib in seasoning.
3. Flip and season the fat cap side of the prime rib.
4. Pre-heat smoker to 225°F.
5. Add prime rib directly to grates, fat cap up.
6. Smoke prime rib at 40 minutes per pound (About 8 hrs for a 15 lb. prime rib). Remove when internal temp reaches 135°F.
7. Let rest for 30 minutes, then slice, serve and enjoy!

Certified Creole Ynot Beef N' Bacon Jerky

Cooking Time: 4 Hrs

Ingredients:

- Bottom Flat Steak- 1 Pound
- Skirt Steak- 1 Pound
- Bacon- 12 ounces
- Kikkoman Teriyaki Baste and Glaze- 11.8 ounce bottle
- Char-Griller Grills Steak Rub
- Pepper Flakes
- Olive Oil
- Large Ziplock Bag
- Fogo Charcoal The Rub
- Fogo Charcoal Eucalyptus & Premium Blends
- Apple Wood Chunks

Directions:

1. Prepping:Slice the Bottom Flat Steak & Skirt Steak into small-medium personal pieces & set aside.Tip: cut small end pieces & excess fat.
2. Pour Kikkoman Teriyaki Baste & Glaze in Ziplock Bag.
3. Apply Olive Oil & Char-griller Grills Steak Rub to both sides of the meat & place in ziplock bag.
4. Mix the meat in the Ziplock bag & place in the refrigerator for 2-24 hours.
5. Remove from fridge and place on tray and allow the meat to get to room temperature.
6. Bacon: No need to marinade. When your ready to cook apply olive oil on both sides of the bacon & season both sides with Fogo Charcoal The Rub.Tip: placing the bacon to a baking rack allows easy handing/rotating of the bacon during the cooking process.
7. Cooking:Preheat smoker/grill with charcoal & apple wood chunks to 180°-200°.Tip: don't allow temperature to rise over 200°. Add charcoal/wood chunks as needed. Low smoke is needed to help dry out the meat. Check fire about

30-45 mins. Tip: do not use a spritz because the goal is to dry out the meat.

8. It will roughly take four hours to cook the jerky. dry out the meat.

9. Jerky will be dark in color, tender & a bit crispy when completed.

10. Dry out the meat.

11. When done, remove jerky from the smoker/grill and enjoy your Beef n' Bacon Jerky throughout the week with Family & Friends.

12. Store jerky in a ziplock bag. No need to place in refrigerator but can if you like.

Spaghetti Stuffed Meatloaf

Cooking Time: 3 Hrs

Ingredients:

- 3 lbs. ground beef
- 1 C. grated parmesan cheese
- 4 eggs lightly beaten
- 2 C. oatmeal or bread crumbs
- 3/4 C. milk
- 3 cloves of garlic minced
- 1 Tsp. pepper
- 2 Tsp. salt
- 2 C. colby jack cheese
- 1/2 to 1 lbs spaghetti
- 1 jar spaghetti sauce

Directions:

1. Mix meatloaf ingredients
2. Add to ground beef & mix well.
3. Cook spaghetti, drain, then add 2 Tbsp. butter. Let cool.
4. Form bottom part of meatloaf and create a bowl shape.
5. Add spaghetti, sauce and 1/3 of Colby cheese.
6. Place the top part of meatloaf on top and work until closed all around.
7. Place on smoker set at 250°F.

8. Cook for 1.25 - 1.5 hours. 9. Pour sauce on top of meatloaf. 10. Smoke for 20 minutes, then add rest of cheese and cook until melted.

9. Smoke for 2 hours or until internal temperature reaches 160°F.

10. Let cool, then slice and serve!

Homemade Grilled Meatballs

Cooking Time: 10 Min

Ingredients:

- 1 Pound of Ground Beef(Chicken or Turkey)
- 2 Large Eggs
- 1/2 Cup of Breadcrumbs
- 1/2 Cup of White Onion(Chopped)
- 1/2 Cup of Grated Romano or Parmesan Cheese
- 1 Tbsp of Minced Garlic
- 1 Tbsp of Dried or Fresh Finely Chopped Parsley
- 1 Tbsp of Dried or Fresh Finely Chopped Basil
- 1 Tsp of Crushed Red Pepper Flakes
- Salt and Pepper to Taste
- Extra Virgin Olive Oil

Directions:

1. In a bowl, combine ground meat, eggs, breadcrumbs, onion, cheese, garlic, parsley, basil, and red pepper flakes. Mix thoroughly then roll meat into meatballs (1-1 ½ inch diameter) Line meatballs on a tray in a single layer and season all over with salt and pepper. Heat grill to medium-high heat and be sure grates are oiled. Brush meatballs with olive oil and place on the grill. Cook until meatballs are browned and cooked throughout for about 10 minutes total, 5 minutes per side. Serve hot, with dipping sauce of choice. Enjoy!

Coffee & Cocoa Tri-tip

Cooking Time: 2 Hrs

Ingredients:
- 2-3 Lb Tri-Tip
- 4 Tbsp Coffee Rub
- 1 Tbsp Unsweetened Cocoa Powder
- Salt to Taste
- 1 tsp Olive Oil

Directions:
1. Remove all excess fat and silver skin from the tri-tip.
2. Mix together all the dry ingredients in a shaker until they are well blended.
3. Use the olive oil as a slather on both sides of the tri-tip to help get the rub to stick. Carefully season both sides and ensure that the tri-tip has a nice even coat of seasoning.
4. Start prepping your fire and working on getting your smoker up to 275 F. Once your smoker has reached 275 F it is time to put the tri-tip on.
5. Once the tri-tip has reached an internal temperature of 125 F it is time to take it out of the smoker and prep for the sear.
6. Place the tri-tip in a pan and cover with foil while you begin to get the grill up to 450-500 F.
7. Tip: You can get a good sear on either the grill or a cast iron skillet.
8. Once the grill has reached 450-500 F place the tri-tip directly on the grill and sear both sides till internal temp reaches 135 F.
9. Pull the tri-tip off the grill and let rest for 15-20 minutes before slicing.
10. Tip: Internal temp for beef varies by preference so feel free to pull it sooner for rare or later for well done.
11. Slice the tri-tip against the grain. Enjoy!

Leftover Brisket Nachos

Cooking Time: 20 Min

Ingredients:
- Tortilla Chips
- Leftover Brisket
- Shredded Cheddar and Monterey Jack Cheese
- Heavy Cream
- Canned Diced Chilis
- Sour Cream
- Limes
- Pickled Jalapenos
- Black Beans
- Avocados
- Radish
- Pico De Gallo: Tomatoes, Onion, Jalapeno, Cilantro

Directions:
1. Prepare your pico de gallo and guacamole
2. Combine diced tomato, jalapeno, onion and cilantro in a bowl and mix with salt and pepper and lime juice
3. Mash 2 avocados together and combine with ½ cup of the pico for some easy guacamole
4. In a skillet prepare the cheese sauce by adding 3 cups shredded cheese and 2 cans of diced chilis. Slowly mix in ½ cup heavy cream and stir until smooth
5. Reheat your leftover brisket in another skillet
6. On a large cookie sheet begin layering your nachos
7. Chips, brisket, black beans, cheese sauce, more chips, brisket, beans cheese sauce.
8. ALWAYS double layer the nachos when possible
9. Top with pico de gallo, pickled jalapenos, sour cream, and guacamole!
10. Garnish with radish and lime wedges and enjoy!

Burnt Ends And Tips

Cooking Time: 1 Hrs

Ingredients:

* 15-18 lb. beef brisket, cooked
* Original All-Purpose BBQ rub or preferred rub, to taste
* 2 C. BBQ sauce
* 1 C. beef broth
* ½ C. garlic wine vinegar
* Extra beef broth for injection and misting

Directions:

1. Smoke brisket the day before.
2. Trim the fat from the brisket leaving an even, thin layer on the top.
3. Season the brisket generously with Original All-Purpose BBQ rub, or your favorite rub, on all sides to your taste.
4. Inject the brisket with the extra beef broth, reserving some for misting. Place brisket fat side up in the smoker for 3 hours at 250°F, with wood chips/chunks, if desired. 5. Open the smoker after 3 hours and inject the brisket with more beef broth, without turning it and mist the exposed surface generously. 6. Remove brisket when internal temperature reaches 160°F, wrap tightly in foil and return to grill.
5. Brisket is done when internal temperature reaches 204°F. Burnt ends and tips
6. Cut the cooked brisket into bite-sized chunks and place into an aluminum roasting pan.
7. Add BBQ sauce, 1 C. beef broth and vinegar to pan and mix well.
8. Place pan on the grill at 300°F for 1 hour or until meat is heated through and sauce has caramelized.

Lou's Beef Brisket

Cooking Time: 10-12 Hrs

Ingredients:

* 15-18 lb. beef brisket
* ½ C. coarse ground pepper
* ½ C. Kosher salt
* Beef broth for injection

Directions:

1. Use the rub ingredients to sprinkle the brisket on all sides to your taste
2. Inject the brisket with the combined ingredients of the injection
3. Use half the combined ingredients for injection and other half for misting
4. Add in your favorite wood chips/chunks (hickory, cherry, etc.)
5. Place brisket onto your smoker, fat side up
6. Cook for three hours in the smoker at 250°F, open it and inject again without turning the brisket 8. Use some of the inject to mist the exposed surface generously 9. Remove brisket when internal temperature reaches 160°F and wrap tightly in foil 10. Return brisket to grill and cook until the internal meat temperature reaches 204°F 11. Remove from heat and allow it to rest for an hour before slicing and serving

Dry Aged Rib Roast

Cooking Time: 1.5 Hrs

Ingredients:

* 6-8 lb. dry aged rib roast
* ½ C. melted butter
* 4 sprigs of parsley
* 4 sprigs of basil
* 4 sprigs of rosemary
* Kosher salt

- Black pepper
- Paprika
- Garlic

Directions:

1. Finely chop parsley, basil, and rosemary, and mix with melted butter

2. Place rib roast on grill at 350°F over indirect heat and grill for approximately 45 minutes

3. Brush roast with buttered herbs

4. Continue to cook over indirect heat for additional 45 minutes or until internal temp reaches 145°F

Reverse Sear Ribeye

Cooking Time: 1 Hrs

Ingredients:

- 1½" thick Ribeye steaks
- Steak BBQ rub, or preferred seasoning, to taste
- Salt and pepper, to taste

Directions:

1. Allow steaks to come to room temperature, then rinse and pat dry with paper towel. Season steaks generously with Steak BBQ rub or preferred seasoning on both sides. Add salt and pepper if needed.

2. Place on the grill to smoke at 170°F for an hour; pull steaks off and set aside to rest.

3. While steaks are resting, increase grill temperature to 400°F.

4. Place steaks back on the grill and sear at 400°F for 5 minutes per side, with a quarter turn at 2½ minutes for good sear marks. Steaks are done when the meat reaches an internal temperature of 140°-145°F for medium-rare.

5. Note: The steak's internal temperature will continue to increase by 5-10 degrees after you pull it off the grill.

Lou's Beef Plate Ribs

Cooking Time: 7 Hrs

Ingredients:

- 1 rack, three bones, Beef Plate Ribs (approx. 6-9 pounds)
- ½ C. coarse ground black pepper
- ¼ C. Kosher salt
- 2 C. beef broth

Directions:

1. Sprinkle liberally with the salt and black pepper mixture, coating lightly over all sides

2. Pre-heat your grill to 275°F

3. Place the ribs on the top rack and smoke for 6 hours at 275°F

4. Mist about every 2 hours with some beef broth in a spray bottle

5. At the end of the 6 hours remove from the smoker and allow to rest for 30 minutes to an hour, then cut and serve

Inch-thick Onion Char-burgers

Cooking Time: 15 Min

Ingredients:

- Angus Ground Beef 85% Lean - 1.5 lbs
- White Bread with Crust Removed - 2 slices
- Milk - 1/4 cup
- Kosher Salt - 1 tsp
- Coarse Ground Pepper - 1/2 tsp
- 1 Clove Garlic - Minced
- Half Large Sweet Onion - Chopped
- Paprika - 1/2 tsp
- Parsley - 1/2 tsp
- Garlic Powder - 1/2 tsp

- Cumin - 1 tsp
- Chili Powder - 1 tsp
- Melted and Cooled Bacon Grease - 3 to 4 Tbsp
- Vegetable Shortening - 1 tsp

Directions:

1. If you have bacon grease on hand, melt 3-4 tbsp in a skillet and set aside to let cool slightly. If you do not have bacon grease, fry 6-8 slices of bacon and spoon 3-4 tbsp aside to let cool slightly.

2. Next you'll want to prep your bread paste. Take the 2 slices of uncrusted white bread and break into small 1/2" pieces and place into small bowl. Add milk and let sit for 5 minutes. Mash down with fork until a paste forms. Set aside.

3. Place ground beef into large mixing bowl. Add salt, pepper, paprika, cumin, parsley, chili powder, garlic powder, minced garlic, chopped fresh onion, bread paste, and slightly cooled bacon grease.

4. Use gloved hands to mix all ingredients evenly into the ground beef. Divide into 4 even portions and form into balls. Flatten each ball to form inch-thick patties. Make center of patties thinner because it will rise as it cooks.

5. Add one fully lit chimney of coals to your favorite Char-Griller charcoal grill. This is a direct, high-heat cook.

6. Place 12" cast-iron skillet on grill grates and close lid. Allow 5-10 minutes to allow skillet to get nice and hot. Add vegetable shortening to ensure a non-stick sear.

7. Place patties in skillet. Sear 1 minute per side.

8. Remove skillet and carefully place patties on AKORN grates directly over coals. Grill 8-11 minutes flipping once.

9. For best results, monitor temp with instant thermometer. For medium-well, pull burgers off the grill at 150° F.

10. Let rest 5-10 minutes.

11. (Optional) While burgers rest, place 12" cast-iron skillet back on grill and fry your eggs with lid closed. Make sure not to over cook, you want a firm egg, but a "drippy" yolk on the inside. Sunny side up.

12. Add burger patty to your bun, top with egg, and your favorite toppings and get ready for one of the juiciest, thickest, and most flavorful burgers you've ever had!

Grilled Caesar Salad

Cooking Time: 20 Min

Ingredients:
- 2 Beef Strip Loin Steaks
- Olive oil
- Salt and pepper to taste
- 2-3 romaine hearts
- 1.5 C. parmesan cheese
- Lemon, halved
- Your favorite caesar dressing

Directions:

1. Rub steaks front and back with olive oil

2. Add salt and pepper to both sides and set aside

3. Cut the ends off 2-3 romaine hearts

4. Then slice in half longways to allow for easy grilling

5. In a cast iron pan add 1½ C. parmesan cheese

6. Preheat grill to 350°F

7. Grill steak for 5-7 per side

8. Cook the cheese in the pan for 8-10 minutes or until golden brown

9. Once ready, remove and flip onto ceramic bowl and let cool

10. Grill the 2-3 romaine hearts for 2-4 minutes

11. Spritz lemon over the romaine hearts

12. Once done, chop up the romaine hearts and place in the cooled parmesan cheese bowl

13. Add your favorite Caesar dressing

Peppered Sirloin With Bacon-mushroom Sauce

Cooking Time: 2 Hrs

Ingredients:

- 12 oz. sirloin steaks, 1-1½" thick
- ½ lb. baby Portabella mushrooms, sliced
- ½ lb. peppered bacon, chopped
- 2 C. beef stock
- 2 Tbsp. all-purpose flour
- 2 Tbsp. minced garlic
- 2 Tsp. Steak BBQ rub

Directions:

1. Fry bacon in batches, if needed, in a pan to desired crispness according to package directions, drain grease and chop when cool. Set aside in a medium bowl. Do not wipe pan. 2. Add mushrooms to the same pan and sauté until tender, 5-7 minutes. Add to bowl with bacon and mix well. Do not wipe pan. 3. Add flour to pan from bacon and mushrooms and whisk into bacon grease. Add garlic and sauté 30-45 seconds, until fragrant. Slowly pour in beef broth and stir continuously to thicken sauce. 4. Add in mushrooms and bacon and stir to incorporate. 5. Transfer all ingredients to cast iron skillet with beans and mix well. 6. Remove pan from heat and set aside.

2. Sirloin

3. Rinse sirloin and pat dry with paper towel. Season sirloin generously on both sides with Steak BBQ rub, or your favorite rub and let rest until meat reaches room temperature. 2. Place sirloin directly on the grill at 400°F for 12 minutes per side, rotating a quarter turn halfway through for good sear marks on each side. Meat is done when internal temperature reaches 140°F for medium-rare. Remove sirloin from grill and allow to rest for 8-10 minutes before slicing.

4. Serve with bacon-mushroom sauce and enjoy!

Double Stack Cheeseburger

Cooking Time: 15 Min

Ingredients:

- 1 lb. ground beef
- Beef/steak all-purpose sauce
- Steak BBQ rub
- 1 sweet onion, sliced
- 1 tomato, sliced
- 2 slices cheddar or pepper jack cheese
- Hamburger buns
- Condiments of choice

Directions:

1. Place ground beef in large bowl and season to taste with Steak BBQ rub or your favorite rub, and sauce. Mix by hand until just blended. 2. Form 1" thick patties and place on a wax paper lined tray. Place tray with patties in refrigerator and allow to chill for 10-15 minutes. 3. Place the onion slices on the grill at 400°F for 5-7 minutes, flipping halfway through, until tender. 4. Place chilled patties on the grill at 400°F for 3 minutes per side, with a quarter turn halfway through for good sear marks. 5. Top burgers with grilled onions and cheese. Allow cheese to melt and

stack one burger on top of the other. Burgers are done when internal temperature reaches 165°F.

2. To serve, add more grilled onions and cheese if desired, top with condiments of choice and enjoy!

Smoked Meatloaf

Cooking Time: 2 Hrs

Ingredients:
- 2 Lbs. Ground Beef
- 1/2 Cup of Onion (Minced)
- 1/4 Cup of Garlic (Minced)
- 2 Eggs (Cracked)
- 1 Tsp of Salt
- 1 Tsp of Pepper
- 1 Tsp of Cayenne Pepper
- 3/4 Cup of Bread Crumbs
- 1 Tbsp of Worcestershire Sauce
- 1/2 Cup of Ketchup
- 1/4 Cup of Brown Sugar
- 1 Tbsp Yellow or Dijon Mustard
- 1 Tbsp of BBQ Sauce

Directions:

1. Preheat your smoker to 225-250°F. In a large mixing bowl, combine all of the ingredients(1-9) for the loaf, thoroughly kneading together. Form into desired load shape. Place the meatloaf into the smoker and smoke for 2 hours or until the internal temperature reaches 160°F. Allow to rest for 30 minutes before slicing. Combine the ingredients(10-13) for the sauce thoroughly and apply to the top of the meatloaf once it has begun to cool down. Serve warm. Enjoy!

Flat Iron Griddle Sizzler N' Veggies Sammies

Cooking Time: 10 Min

Ingredients:
- Thinly Sliced Steak or Beef Sizzlers
- 1/2 Onions
- 1 Jalapeño (Sliced)
- Favorite Beef Rub or Seasoning
- Italian Bread
- Olive Oil In Squeeze Bottle
- Beef Bouillon Juice Mixture In A Squeeze Bottle
- Cheddar Cheese (Shredded)

Directions:

1. Slice the green pepper, onions and Jalapeño and place in bowl. Apply olive oil to both sides of the meat as a binder for the seasonings. Apply favorite beef rub/seasoning to both sides of the meat. Heat up your Char-Griller Flat Iron Griddle to medium heat with good portion of olive oil. Add all the veggies and cook for 5 mins before adding the meat. Add meat to the griddle and cook on each side for 3 mins then chop the meat on the griddle into small pieces. Combine the meat and veggies, add some beef bouillon juice mixture to it and cook for 5 minutes. Add cheddar cheese and cook until melted, roughly 2 mins. Toast Italian Bread, then add the cheesy veggie meat to the bread and enjoy!

Corned Beef Brisket And Potatoes

Cooking Time: 5 Hrs

Ingredients:
- 18 lb. corned beef brisket
- 2 Tbsp. cinnamon
- 1 Tbsp. nutmeg
- 2 Tbsp. Allspice
- 3 Tbsp. salt
- 2 Tbsp. minced garlic

- 2 Idaho potatoes
- 6 oz. shredded cheese of your choice
- 6 oz. heavy cream
- 2 oz. chopped shallot
- Salt and pepper
- 2 oz. peppercorn

Directions:

1. Mix peppercorn, cinnamon, nutmeg, Allspice, salt and garlic.
2. Add vinegar based BBQ sauce to brisket.
3. Add spice mix all over the brisket on both sides.
4. Heat smoker to 225°F.
5. Smoke brisket until internal temp reaches 165°F.
6. Heat butter in a cast iron skillet
7. Add chopped shallot.
8. Chop and boil Idaho potatoes for 10 minutes in water.
9. Add salt and pepper to taste.
10. Add heavy cream to potatoes.
11. Close grill and bring to a boil.
12. Add your favorite shredded cheese
13. Mix well and cook for another 10-15 minutes.

Akorn Dino Beef Plate Ribs

Cooking Time: 5 Hours Min

Ingredients:

- Beef Plate Ribs
- Mustard
- Loot N' Booty What's Your Beef Rub
- 50/50 Coarse Salt & Coarse Pepper
- Akorn Kamado Charcoal Grill
- Smokin' Stone & Drip Pan
- Fogo Premium Lump Charcoal & Mesquite Wood Chunks
- Char-Griller Grills Remote Thermometer
- Butcher Paper
- Apple Juice With Spritzer

Directions:

1. Smoked Beef Ribs are full of flavor and are easy to make.
2. pounds beef plate bone ribs (3 bones): Trim fat and silver skin from the top and bottom. Apply mustard to all the sides. Season all sides of the meat with Loot N' Booty What's Your Beef Rub and 50/50 Coarse Salt & Coarse Pepper. Tip: Allow ribs to get to room temperature prior to smoking. This allows the seasonings to sweat and absorb into the meat and meat to start smoking faster. Prep Akorn Kamado Charcoal Grill, Smokin' Stone & drip pan filled with water. Preheat Akorn Kamado & Smoke at temperature 250°: used Fogo Premium Lump Charcoal & Mesquite Wood Chunks. Tip: remember to use your Char-Griller Grills Remote Thermometer to take the guess work out your cooking. Spritz with apple juice every 45 minutes during the smoking process and rotate the ribs each time. Place ribs in Akorn Kamado and smoke until internal temperature 170° is met, roughly takes 4-5 hours. Tip: while smoking if a spot on the meat is getting too much char, place a small piece of foil covering the spot to help prevent that spot from burning/drying out. Wrap with peach/butcher paper and apple juice once internal temperature 170° is met. Place back in the Akorn Kamado and cook until internal temperature 199° is met, roughly takes one-two hours. Remove from the smoker and allow to rest in a cooler covered with a towel/blanket for 1-2 hours. Remove, slice and enjoy!

Pastrami Swiss Burger

Cooking Time: 40 Min

Ingredients:
- 2 lbs. ground beef
- ½ lb. Pastrami, sliced
- 2 eggs, beaten
- Steak BBQ rub
- 1 C. beef all-purpose sauce
- Swiss cheese, sliced
- Hamburger buns
- Condiments of choice

Directions:

1. Place ground beef in large bowl, add eggs and season with Steak BBQ rub, or your favorite rub, to taste and sauce. Mix ingredients by hand until just blended.

2. Form 1" thick patties and place on a wax paper lined tray. Place tray with patties in refrigerator and allow to chill for 10-15 minutes.

3. Place chilled patties on the grill at 350°F for 5 minutes per side, with a quarter turn halfway through for good sear marks.

4. Bush burgers with more sauce, if desired and top with sliced pastrami and cheese. Allow cheese to melt, about 1-2 minutes. Burgers are done when internal temperature reaches 165°F for medium-rare.

Over The Top Chili On The Grand Champ

Ingredients:
- 1 Pound of 80/20 Ground Beef
- 1 Pound of Hot (or your favorite) Italian Sausage
- 1 Pound of your favorite Bacon
- 1 Large Yellow Onion (Diced)
- 1 Green Bell Pepper (Diced)
- 1 Yellow Bell Pepper (Diced)
- 3 Cloves of Garlic (Minced)
- 15 oz Can of Red Kidney Beans- Drained (Not rinsed)
- 15 oz Can of Black Beans- Drained (Not rinsed)
- 29 oz Can of Yellow Sweet Corn Kernels- Drained (Not rinsed)
- 14.5 oz Can of Diced Tomatoes with Green Chiles (Kind of like a can of Rotel)
- 3 oz of Tomato Paste
- 1 Tbsp of Chili Powder
- 1 Tbsp of Paprika
- 2 Tsp of Onion Powder
- 1 Tsp of Black Pepper
- 3/4 Tsp of Salt
- 1 Tsp of Cayenne Pepper
- 2 Cups of Beef Broth

Directions:

1. In a large bowl, mix the ground beef and Italian sausage together well. Mix in the Paprika, Salt, Pepper, Cayenne, Cumin, Chili Powder and Onion Powder to the meat. Mix well with your hands or use a mixer! Place seran wrap or foil over the bowl with the meat and place in fridge to relax... In a medium/large skillet (I prefer cast iron skillets) lightly oil the skillet and set heat to medium high. Add in your onion and bell peppers and cook until the onions become translucent and just start to develop some color. Add in your 3 cloves of minced garlic. Cook until fragrant. Remove skillet from heat and put aside (I dumped the veggies into the chili pot at this point). Cook your bacon in the same skillet to your liking... I suggest you don't over cook your bacon. You don't want it crispy for the chili. It

will continue to cook once on the smoker/in the cooker. When bacon is to your liking, add it to the pot with the onion and bell peppers. Add the remaining ingredients to your pot. The cans of beans/tomatoes, corn, beef broth, Worcestershire sauce, etc.... Time to fire up the smoker/cooker!

2. Tip: Make the meat into a ball by using seran wrap!! So much easier!

3. Place the pot on the bottom rack or ash pan grates of your cooker/smoker. Place the "meatball" on the grate directly above the pot of chili. Cook at 275 degrees F (135 Celsius) until the meatball reaches an internal temperature of 165 degrees F (74 Celsius). Remove both the pot and the meat. Cover the meat loosely in foil to allow to rest and reabsorb all those juices. Once rested, break apart and crumble (to the size of your liking) the meat ball into the pot of chili. Mix well and serve with some shredded cheese and sour cream, perhaps even some oyster crackers!!

Chili Jalapeño Burger

Cooking Time: 10 Min

Ingredients:

- ½ C. mayonnaise
- ½ Tsp. ground white pepper
- 1 Tsp. garlic powder
- 1 Tsp. Chipotle chili powder
- 2 lbs. ground beef
- 2 eggs, beaten
- 1 ½ C. all-purpose beef sauce (reserve ½ C.)
- 1 Tbsp. Steak BBQ rub
- 15 oz. can chili, preferred (without beans)
- 2-3 jalapeños, sliced
- Hamburger buns
- Cheddar cheese slices
- Condiments of choice

Directions:

1. Combine the mayonnaise, white pepper, garlic powder, Chipotle chili powder and ½ C. of reserved sauce in a small bowl. Mix thoroughly. 2. Cover with plastic wrap and place it in the refrigerator for 30 minutes to chill.

2. Ground beef

3. Place ground beef in large bowl, add eggs and season with 1 Tbsp. Steak BBQ rub, or your favorite rub, to taste and remaining sauce. Mix ingredients by hand until just blended. 2. Form 1" thick patties and place on a wax paper lined tray. Place tray with patties in refrigerator and allow to chill for 10-15 minutes. Prepare chili according to package directions. Set aside. 4. Place chilled patties on the grill at 350°F for 5 minutes per side, with a quarter turn halfway through for good sear marks. 5. Top burgers with cheese and allow to melt. Burgers are done when internal temperature reaches 165°F.

4. To serve, place a spoonful of chili on each burger and top with jalapeño slices. For another layer of flavor, spread Chipotle mayonnaise on top of the hamburger bun.

PORK

Certified Grilled And Smoked Baby Back Ribs

Cooking Time: 2 1/2 Hrs

Ingredients:

- Full Slabs of Spare Ribs.
- Hot Sauce
- Favorite BBQ Rub
- Favorite BBQ Sauce
- Apple Juice (Non Concentrate)

Directions:

1. Trimming
2. Using a sharp knife slice remove any meat loose on the ends of the ribs. Also remove any access fat from top/meat side of the ribs. Tip: If you can pull any fat, you should remove it.
3. Flip the ribs over so the bones are facing up. Remove the membrane and discard. Remove any access fat.
4. Seasoning
5. Begin by leaving the the ribs bone side up. Apply coating of hot sauce for a binder. Tip: don't apply hot sauce or rubs on the sides of the ribs. This helps the exposed bones from getting burnt during the smoking process.
6. Apply even coating of BBQ rubs on the ribs.
7. Flip ribs to the top/meat side of the ribs. Apply coating of hot sauce for a binder. Tip: seasoning the bottom of the ribs first will help prevent the top/meat side seasonings from being messy.
8. Apply an even coating of BBQ rub on the top of the ribs.
9. Ribs are ready to be Smoked.

10. Grilling & Smoking
11. Grill the ribs for 2 minutes on the meat side down on the grill grill grate. Reverse them after one minute.
12. Flip the ribs so they meat side is facing up and grill for an additional 1-2 minutes.
13. Using your Char-Griller Grill glove and grill grate lifter, lift the grill grate and move off to the side of the grill. Quickly insert the Char-Griller Akorn Smokin' stone, insert Char-Griller grill drip pan filled with water, place grill grate with meat back in the pit.
14. Shut the top smoke stack to a low setting and dodge same to the bottom of the vent. This will allow you to quickly lower your fire. Lock in the temperature when it hits temperature 325°-350° by adjusting the smoke stack and bottom vent.
15. Spritz with apple juice every 30 minutes and rotate ribs.
16. After smoking for 2 1/2 hours coat ribs with BBQ sauce and smoke for an additional 20 minutes.
17. Remove Ribs and allow to rest for 15 minutes. Slice and enjoy.

Apple Chipotle Glazed Smoked Ham

Cooking Time: 90 Min

Ingredients:

- 5 ½ lbs. boneless Applewood smoked ham
- 1 C. apple jelly
- 1 Tsp. Chipotle chili powder
- 2/3 C. balsamic vinegar
- ½ C. brown sugar

Directions:

1. Place ham in an aluminum roasting pan onto the grill to smoke at 300°F for 90 minutes.

2. While ham is smoking, combine balsamic vinegar, brown sugar, Chipotle chili powder and apple jelly in a small sauce pan on the stove. Bring to a boil, then reduce heat and simmer for 15 minutes, stirring occasionally.

3. After ham has cooked for 1 hour, baste with glaze every 10 minutes, being careful not to burn the sauce. Ham is done when internal temperature reaches 140°F.

4. Remove ham from grill and let rest for 10 minutes before slicing and serving.

Gravity 980 Smoked Pork Shoulder

Cooking Time: 3-4 Hrs

Ingredients:

- 1 7-9 Lb. Pork Shoulder, trimmed
- 3 Tbsp of Yellow Mustard
- 2 Tbsp Kosher Salt
- 2 Tbsp Black Pepper
- 2 Tbsp Garlic Powder
- 2 Tbsp Onion Powder
- 1 Tbsp Paprika
- 1 Tbsp Cumin
- 1 Cup of Apple Juice or Apple Cider Vinegar
- 1/2 Cup of Water

Directions:

1. No more babysitting your pork shoulder with the Gravity 980. Easily prepare an awesome pork shoulder for stellar dishes like sandwiches, mac and cheese or even nachos.

2. In a small bowl, combine seasonings, and in a spray, bottle combine apple cider/juice and water. Thoroughly rub mustard all over the surface of your pork shoulder then coat with all the seasonings. Remove the fire shutter from your Gravity 980 then light and load the hopper. Set the temperature to 225-250°F. Place your pork shoulder on the grill, close the lid and smoke it for 3 hours without opening the lid. Spray the shoulder generously with spray bottle mixture then continue to do so every hour for the next 3-4 hours until the shoulder reaches 200-205°F. Optionally, once the fat on top splits open, you may wrap the shoulder in butcher paper or aluminum foil for the duration of the cook. Remove from the smoker and allow it to rest for 1 hour before removing the bone and shredding. Enjoy!

Blueberry Pork Belly Burnt Ends

Cooking Time: 3.5 Hrs

Ingredients:

- Pork Belly - 2 lbs
- Char-Griller Rib Rub
- Butter - 1/2 stick
- Fresh Blueberries - 2 Cups
- Apple Juice - 1/4 Cup
- Sugar - 1/4 Cup
- Cornstarch - 1 Tbs
- Lemon Juice - 1 Tbs
- Cayenne - 1 tsp (optional)

Directions:

1. Cut the pork belly into 1-1 ½ inch cubes.

2. Season the cubes liberally on all sides.

3. Prepare the fire to get the smoker up to 275 F.

4. Tip: Put the pork belly into the freezer 20-30 minutes before you cube. This will help with the cutting process.

5. Once the smoker has reached 275 F put the pork belly onto the grill with the fat side facing down.

6. Spritz every 40-45 minutes until the pork belly starts to read an internal temp of 190 F.

7. Place the cubes in an aluminum pan and add one cup of the blueberry sauce and the butter. Toss the cubes to make sure the sauce adheres to all sides of the cubes. Return the pan into the smoker.

8. Once the sauce has reduced and the cubes look caramelized it is time to pull from the smoker. Put the burnt ends onto a plate and top with the remaining cup of blueberry sauce. Enjoy!

9. In a saucepan combine the blueberries and apple juice. Bring to a boil. Pour the cornstarch, sugar, and cayenne (optional) into the saucepan while stirring continuously. Let the sauce thicken and reduce heat. Add the lemon juice and stir. Set aside till it is time to use on the burnt ends.

10. Serving Suggestion: Over Homemade Waffles

Bacon Wrapped Kielbasa

Cooking Time: 1 Hrs

Ingredients:
- Smoked sausage or kielbasa
- 2-3 jalapeños, cored and sliced
- Block of Colby jack or pepper jack cheese, cut into thick slices
- Package of bacon
- Original All-Purpose BBQ Rub, to taste
- Favorite BBQ sauce for dipping

Directions:
1. Cut sausage into ½ inch thick slices. Place a slice of cheese on top, then a slice of jalapeño.
2. Wrap with 2 slices of bacon on opposite sides.

3. Season with Original All-Purpose BBQ rub, or your favorite rub, to taste.
4. Heat grill to 300°F. Place bacon-wrapped kielbasa on the grill and smoke for around 1 hour.
5. Let cool, then serve with your favorite BBQ sauce for dipping!

Bone-in Pulled Ham

Cooking Time: 8 Hrs

Ingredients:
- 12-15 lb. bone-in ham
- 2-20 oz. cans of crushed pineapple
- 4 C. brown sugar
- 6 Tbsp. mustard

Directions:
1. Get smoker ready and set at 250°F.
2. Place ham in an aluminum pan or cast-iron Dutch oven
3. Divide marinade in half, and pour one half marinade over top of ham
4. Place ham in smoker and baste hourly
5. Cook for around 8 1/2 hours, until ham reaches internal temp of 160°F
6. Remove ham from smoker and cover with foil for 1-2 hours
7. Shred ham and place in slow cooker or stock pot, adding juice and drippings from pan
8. Add additional marinade and pour over top of ham, mixing well
9. Cook for 1 hour until marinade is fully incorporated into shredded ham
10. All done! Makes good sandwiches or great to eat alone!

Bacon Wrapped Kabob

Cooking Time: 10 Min

Ingredients:

- 1 Lb KC Cattle Company (Wagyu Stew or Kabob Meat)
- 10 Strips of Bacon (Cut In Half)
- 1 Tsp Redmond Real Salt
- 1 Tsp Redmond Organic Garlic Pepper

Directions:

1. Season beef with salt & pepper, wrap each piece with bacon & skewer them. Cook on flat iron griddle (or grill) turning every 2 minutes, for 10 minutes. I finished mine off in the air fryer to crisp the bacon up a little more without over cooking the beef.

Pork Belly Street Tacos

Cooking Time: 4 Hrs

Ingredients:

- Pork Belly - 2 to 3 lbs
- 1 Tbsp Salt
- 2 Tbsp Coarse Black Pepper
- 1 Tbsp Yellow Mustard
- 1/2 Cup Apple Cider Vinegar
- 1/2 Cup Water
- Tortillas, Onion, Cilantro

Directions:

1. Prep your Char-Griller offset smoker to a temp of 275 F. Unwrap the pork belly and trim any excess fat or meat that is not needed. *Tip* to achieve that true Central Texas Style flavor try to use oak chunks or splits throughout your cook.

2. Combine all dry ingredients in shaker for easy application. Rub the pork belly down with mustard or a binder of your choice. Season the pork belly liberally.

3. Put the pork belly on the smoker once it is seasoned and the smoker temperature is at 275 F.

4. At the hour mark spritz the pork belly with a mixture of apple cider vinegar and water. Continue to spritz every 45 minutes until the pork belly has reached an internal temp of 165 F.

5. Wrap the pork belly in butcher paper once it has reached an internal temp of 165 F.

6. Tip: This will help with rendering the fat and preserving the bark on the pork belly.

7. Once the pork belly has reached an internal temp of around 203 F it is time to take off the pit and let rest so the juices can redistribute. Rest for 30-45 minutes.

8. Chop up the pork belly and serve in a tortilla with cilantro and onions and enjoy!

Pork Belly Burnt Ends On The Akorn

Cooking Time: 2 Hrs

Ingredients:

- Slab of Pork Belly
- BBQ Rub
- 1 Stick Butter
- 1/2 Cup Brown Sugar
- Honey
- BBQ sauce
- 8 oz Apple Juice

Directions:

1. Remove skin from pork belly Cut up pork belly in 5" squares Set smoker to 250-275F - indirect - add cherry wood Place cubed pork belly pieces on smoker - cook for 1.5-2 hours Place pork belly in aluminum pan - pour in brown sugar, honey and pads of your butter Cover, and place in smoker for another 1.5-2hrs (until about 205F) Grab a new pan.. drizzle with glaze(4 oz

apple juice 1 cup of bbq sauce) and shake up so they're covered Return pieces to smoker, uncovered for approx 5-10 mins until tacky Enjoy!

Smoked Pork Shoulder

Ingredients:
- 5 to 7 Pound Pork Shoulder or Boston Butt
- Char-Griller Rib Rub
- Spray Bottle Full of 2/3 Apple Juice and 1/3 Vegetable Oil

Directions:
1. Trim excess fat from the pork shoulder. (Skip this step if it is Boston Butt.) Score the remaining fat with a sharp knife.
2. Rub a liberal amount of Rib Spice Rub on the pork. Make sure each side is evenly coated.
3. Place pork in the fridge for at least 12 hours.
4. Remove pork from fridge one hour before placing on the grill.
5. Preheat offset smoker to 225 to 250 degrees Fahrenheit. Add Apple or Cherry wood chunks to coals.
6. Place drip pan filled with water under the grates. Place pork on the grates over the drip pan.
7. Baste pork with Apple juice every 30 to 60 minutes.
8. Make sure to keep an eye on the pit temperature. Add more pre-lit charcoal to the Side Fire Box if needed.
9. Smoke until internal temperature is 195 to 210 degrees Fahrenheit and remove from grill.

Pork Tenderloin Sliders

Cooking Time: 8-10 Min

Ingredients:
- (2) 1 lb. pork tenderloins
- Salt and pepper, to taste
- Olive oil, for brushing
- Slider buns

Directions:
1. Pre-heat grill to 400°F. Rinse tenderloins and pat dry with paper towel. 2. Generously season with salt and pepper or use Original All-Purpose BBQ rub, to taste. 3. Place pork tenderloins on the grill at 400°F for 4 minutes per side, brushing with olive oil occasionally, and turning to ensure good sear marks on each side. Pork is done when internal temperature reaches 140°F. 4. Toast slider buns for 1-2 minutes before serving.
2. Brush with a layer of BBQ sauce and allow pork to rest for 10 minutes before slicing and serving on toasted slider buns.

Raspberry Chipotle Glazed Pork Tenderloin

Cooking Time: 35 Min

Ingredients:
- 2 Lb Pork Tenderloin
- 1 tsp Mustard
- 1 Tbsp Char-Griller Rib Rub
- 3/4 Cup Raspberry Chipotle BBQ Sauce

Directions:
1. Pre-heat the grill to 325 F and set up for cooking with indirect heat
2. Trim excess fat off the pork tenderloin.
3. Rub down with a light coating of mustard to help the rub stick.
4. Season all sides of the pork tenderloin with Char-Griller Rib Rub
5. Once the grill has reached 325 F place the pork tenderloin on the grill in indirect heat.

6. Once the pork tenderloin has reached an internal temp of 140 F it is time to apply the glaze.

7. Heat up the raspberry chipotle sauce and use a brush to apply the glaze on the pork tenderloin.

8. Once the glaze has set and the internal temp of the pork tenderloin has reached 145 F it is time to pull off the grill and let rest for 10 minutes.

9. Slice and serve with extra raspberry chipotle sauce for dipping. Enjoy!

Simple Smoked Bbq Pork Belly

Cooking Time: 2.5 Hrs

Ingredients:

* Redmond's Pink Himalayan Salt- 1 Teaspoon
* Redmond's Organic Garlic Pepper- 1 Teaspoon
* Butter- 1 stick
* G Hughes Sweet & Spicy BBQ Sauce-1/4-1/2 Cup

Directions:

1. Pat pork belly dry with paper towel
2. Season to taste with Pink salt & garlic pepper
3. Baste with bbq sauce
4. Smoke at 250° in aluminum pan with butter for 2.5 hours. Then place directly over the coals for 5 minutes
5. Add more BBQ glaze if desired.

Brown Sugar Glazed Smoked Ham

Cooking Time: 2 Hrs

Ingredients:

* 11 lb. ham
* 1 C. brown sugar
* 1 C. brown mustard, or preferred

Directions:

1. Combine brown sugar and mustard together in a small bowl to make glaze. Mix well.

2. Score ham in a diamond pattern and generously brush on glaze.

3. Place glazed ham in large baking dish or cast-iron skillet onto the grill to smoke at 325°F for 2 hours. Ham is done when internal temperature reaches 140°F.

4. Remove ham from grill and let rest for 10 minutes before slicing and serving.

Bacon Bourbon Compound Butter Recipe

Cooking Time: 30 Min

Ingredients:

* Softened Butter - 1 Stick
* Crispy Bacon Crumbled - 1 to 2 Slices
* Bacon Grease - 1 Tablespoon
* Bourbon - 1 Tablespoon

Directions:

1. Thoroughly mix and scoop onto a square of parchment paper, rolling up into a log, and twisting the ends closed.

2. Wrap in plastic wrap and refrigerate until firm.

Bbq Pork Spare Ribs

Ingredients:

* Slab of Ribs- 1
* Mustard- 1/4 Cup
* Char Griller Rib Rub- 4 Tablespoon
* Butter- 1 Stick
* Apple Cider Vinegar- 1/2 Cup
* Jack Stack BBQ Seasoning- 6 Tablespoons

- G Hughes Sweet & Spicy BBQ Sauce (or Preferred BBQ Sauce)- 2/3 Cup

Directions:

1. Pat the ribs dry with a paper towel & tear off the membrane.
2. Rub a layer of mustard over the ribs.
3. Rub the ribs down with Char-Griller Rib Rub (to taste).
4. Rub the ribs down with Jack Stack BBQ seasoning (to taste).
5. Marinate for an hour.
6. Smoke ribs around 225° for 3 hours, bone side down uncovered.
7. Wrap in foil with butter & apple cider vinegar, smoke for 2 more hours.
8. Remove foil & brush with BBQ sauce & place on grill grate bone side down for 1 more hour basting occasionally.

Asian Pork Belly Skewers

Cooking Time: 2 Hrs

Ingredients:

- Pork Belly Cut into 1 1/2" Cubes - 2 Pounds
- Pineapple Cut into 1 1/2" Cubes - 1
- Char-Griller Rib Rub
- Skewers Soaked in Water
- Chopped Green Onions and Sesame Seeds - For Garnish
- Chili Garlic Sauce - 1 Tablespoon
- Rice Wine Vinegar - 1 Teaspoon
- Chopped Garlic - 1 Teaspoon
- Orange Zest - 1 Teaspoon
- Soy Sauce - 2 Teaspoons

Directions:

1. Light grill for indirect heat
2. In a large bowl, toss pork belly with rub until generously coated
3. Skewer pineapple and pork belly, alternating between the two
4. Please skewers on the grill
5. Rotate skewers after an hour
6. Meanwhile, place all sauce ingredients in a small sauce pan
7. Chili Garlic Sauce Rice Wine Vinegar Chopped Garlic Range Zest Soy Sauce Honey Ground Ginger
8. Bring the sauce to a simmer and allow to cook until thickened. Approximately 15 minutes
9. Allow to cool
10. After two hours, brush the skewers with sauce. Allow the sauce to set for approximately 30 minutes
11. When ready to serve, sprinkle with sesame seeds and green onions

Memphis-style Dry Ribs

Cooking Time: 5 Hrs

Ingredients:

- 3 racks of ribs
- Ribs BBQ rub, to taste
- Apple juice
- Brown sugar
- Honey
- 12 oz. bottle of squeeze butter

Directions:

1. Rinse rib racks and pat dry with paper towel. Remove membrane from each rack by carefully prying back using the back of a sharp knife. Discard membrane. Flip racks and trim loose ends and excess fat.
2. Tip: Use a paper towel to help hold the membrane, as it's slippery.
3. Season ribs generously with Ribs BBQ Rub, or your favorite rub.

4. When setting up the grill, use a full chimney of unlit charcoal in the attached Side Fire Box and pour another ½ chimney of hot coals on top to ensure good smoke and a temperature of 275°F. Add Applewood chunks on top.

5. Adjust the charcoal grate to the highest setting in the main compartment. Place an aluminum pan on the grate and fill halfway with apple juice. Smoke ribs for 1 hour and mist with apple juice. Close lid and smoke for another 3 hours.

6. After 3 hours, remove ribs from grill and wrap. Before wrapping, spread a generous layer of brown sugar, butter and honey onto aluminum foil. Place ribs meat side down and wrap securely.

7. Transfer wrapped ribs to the grill and smoke at 275°F for another hour. Carefully drain juices before slicing and serving.

Flavor Pro Smoked Pork Shoulder

Cooking Time: 90 Minutes Per Pound And Then 1 Hour Rest Hrs

Ingredients:

- 5 to 6 Pound Bone-In Pork Shoulder or Boston Butt
- Char-Griller Rib Rub
- Spray Bottle Full of Apple Juice and Oil

Directions:

1. Trim excess fat from the pork shoulder. (Skip this step if it is Boston Butt.) Score the remaining fat with a sharp knife.

2. Rub a liberal amount of Rib Spice Rub on the pork. Make sure each side is evenly coated.

3. Place pork in the fridge for at least 12 hours.

4. Remove pork from fridge one hour before placing on the grill.

5. Cover the left-most and center Wood Product Zones of the Flavor Drawer with foil to catch the grease.

6. Place 15 to 20 charcoal briquettes in the far right side of the Flavor Drawer.

7. Turn the burners on high and ignite. Allow the briquettes to fully ash over.

8. Once the briquettes have ashed over, add two to three wood chunks to the charcoal.

9. To Use a Log: Place a log of no more than 3 inches in diameter and 7 inches long the right-most wood product zone. Light using the right most burner.

10. The log should take about 5 to 6 minutes to ignite.

11. After the log has ignited, turn off the gas burner and allow the grill to preheat.

12. Using a Grilling Glove, adjust the smokestacks until the internal temperature of the pit holds steady at 225.

13. Place the pork over the foil and close the grill.

14. Baste pork with Apple juice every 30 to 60 minutes.

15. Make sure to keep an eye on the pit temperature. Add another log every hour or so.

16. Smoke until internal temperature is 195 to 210 degrees Fahrenheit and remove from grill.

17. Tip: If your pork shoulder hits the dreaded "stall" (won't get above 165 degrees Fahrenheit or starts dropping, wrap it in foil, add some apple juice and place back on the grill. This will get it going again.

18. Allow pork to rest for 30 minutes to an hour for best results.

Grilled Pork Chops

Ingredients:

- 4 Bone-In or Boneless Pork Chops
- 1/4 Cup of Olive Oil
- 2 Tbsp of Soy Sauce
- 1 Tbsp of Worcestershire Sauce
- 1 Tsp of Crushed Red Pepper Flakes
- 1/2 Tsp of Cumin
- 1 Tbsp of Honey
- 1 Tsp of Chopped Parsley
- Kosher Salt
- Ground Black Pepper

Directions:

1. In a bowl, mix the olive oil, soy sauce, Worcestershire sauce, red pepper flakes, cumin, honey and desired amount of salt and pepper. Add the marinade and pork chops to a resealable bag and allow to marinate for 1 hour up to overnight. Heat the grill to medium heat and place each pork chop on the grill, cooking for 6-8 minutes per side or until the internal temperature of the thickest part reaches 145°F. Remove the chops from the grill and allow them to rest for 5-10 minutes before garnishing with parsley and serving with desired sides. Enjoy!

Smoked Pork Loin

Cooking Time: 2 Hrs

Ingredients:

- Pork Loin
- 2 Tbsp Of Your Favorite Rub Of Any Kind

Directions:

1. Remove loin from packaging and remove any silverskin if necessary. Cover the loin in the 2 Tbsp of rub Bring your cooker up to 300 degrees, set it up for indirect cooking and add 1 small piece of hickory wood. Place the pork loin on the grate and place a leave in thermometer in it and set it for 4 degrees. Once the loin hits 145 degrees internal temperature remove it from the cooker, cut it into 1 inch chops and serve

How To: Easy Dry Rub Grilled Pork Tenderloin

Ingredients:

- 1.5 Lbs Pork Tenderloin (Trimmed and Pat Dry)
- 1 Tbsp Brown Sugar
- 1 Tbsp Garlic Powder
- 1 Tbsp Chili Powder
- 1 Tbsp Salt
- 1 Tbsp Black Pepper
- 1 Tsp Smoked Paprika
- 1 Tsp Red Chili Flake

Directions:

1. Preheat Char-Griller Grill to high heat. For an easy weeknight dinner, I use the gas side of my Texas Trio for quick cooking, but of course, charcoal flavor would only add to this recipe! While grill is heating, mix spices together, sprinkle heavily over the meat, and rub well. Allow the meat to sit at room temperature for about 20 minutes, letting the spices marry. When grill has reached high heat, add pork loin and close lid. In 5 minutes, rotate meat clockwise to make diamond marks, and allow to cook another 5 minutes with the lid closed. After 10 minutes on one side has passed, flip your pork, and repeat- 5 minutes in one position with the lid closed, and rotate again, 5 minutes with the lid closed. I like to pull my pork off the grill at 145 degrees. While it rests, it will come up about 5-8 more degrees, allowing the meat to stay perfectly moist. Remove

meat from the grill, cover loosely with foil, and let rest for 15 minutes before slicing. Serve with your favorite grilled vegetable or a large tossed salad. Enjoy!

Smoked Meatballs With Sweet And Sour Sauce

Cooking Time: 30 Min

Ingredients:

- 3/4 Cup Panko Breadcrumbs (Meatballs)
- 1/2 Yellow Onion, Minced (Meatballs)
- 1/2 Pounds 80/20 Ground Beef (Meatballs)
- 1 Egg (Meatballs)
- 2 Garlic Cloves, Minced (Meatballs)
- 1.5 tsp Worcestershire Sauce (Meatballs)
- 1 Tbsp Bacon Fat (Melted, Cooled) (Meatballs)
- 1/2 tsp Kosher Salt (Meatballs)
- 3/4 tsp Black Pepper
- 1 Tbsp Cornstarch (Sauce)
- 1/4 Cup Water (Sauce)
- 1/4 Cup Apple Cider Vinegar (Sauce)
- 1/2 Cup Brown Sugar (Sauce)
- 1/4 Cup Ketchup (Sauce)
- 1 Tbsp Soy Sauce (Sauce)

Directions:

1. Prepare smoker grill for 375°F add mild smoking wood for smoke flavor.

2. In a large mixing bowl, add ground beef, ground pork, melted bacon fat, onion, and breadcrumbs. Mix together with hands to coat. Let sit for a few minutes.

3. Add remaining meatball ingredients and mix with hands to combine.

4. Scoop out level tablespoons of the meat mixture and set on work surface. Roll each in hands to form a smooth meatball.

5. Spray down a racked baking tray with oil. Place meatballs on rack.

6. Bake/smoke for 30 minutes or until browned. Cook to at least 165°F internal temperature. Remove from heat and transfer meatballs to a large bowl immediately to avoid sticking.

7. Combine all ingredients in a small saucepan over medium heat. Whisk to combine.

8. Bring to simmer, stirring frequently. Then simmer until sauce thickens like maple syrup. (3-5 minutes)

9. Cover meatballs with sweet and sour sauce sauce. Transfer to a serving dish with toothpicks and remaining dipping sauce.

10. Keep warm and stir occasionally prior to serving.

11. Enjoy!

Easter Sunday Texas-style Pulled Pork

Cooking Time: 8 Hrs

Ingredients:

- 6 to 7 Lb. Pork Shoulder
- 1/4 C. Kosher Salt
- 1/4 C. Coarse Black Pepper
- 2 Tbsp. Garlic Powder
- 2 Tbsp. Onion Powder
- 2 Tbsp. Paprika
- Hamburger Buns
- 1/2 C. Apple Juice (For Spritz)
- 1/2 C. Water (For Spritz)

Directions:

1. Easter Sunday is a time where we get together with family and friends. And what better way to feed all these people than with some Texas-style pulled pork sandwiches. Pulled pork really isn't a staple in Central-Texas BBQ but we love making

it, and it feeds a lot of people. Your guests will be thanking you as they dive into some savory pork action!

2. Unwrap the pork shoulder and trim any excess fat or meat that may be hanging off.

3. You want to make it aerodynamic so the smoke flows evenly and does not create any burnt pieces.

4. Combine all dry ingredients in shaker for easy application.

5. Rub the pork shoulder down with olive oil or a binder of your choice. Season the pork shoulder liberally.

6. Get your grill up to 275°F and add a water pan to the side closest to the Side Fire Box.

7. This will allow for extra moisture inside the pit.

8. Once your grill is at 275°F you can go ahead and put the pork shoulder on. Let the pit do the work and tend to the fire as needed.

9. Tip: When preparing a fire, I usually use one large chimney of charcoal and add oak splits throughout the cook to maintain temp. The oak gives it that extra flavor you find in Central-Texas BBQ.

10. During the cook time is when I put my coleslaw together. Get the recipe here.

11. At around the 3-hour mark of the cook it is time to take-a-peek at the pork shoulder and spritz with the apple juice/water mixture to get some moisture on it.

12. Also, make sure that your water pan still has plenty of water left in it. Close the lid and keep on cooking.

13. Tip: Try to limit the amount of times you open the pit in order to limit fluctuations in temperature.

14. At around the 5-hour mark it is time to wrap the pork shoulder. Put it in an aluminum pan with some extra apple juice/water mixture to help with moisture.

15. Cover the pan with a layer of foil and put it back in the pit at 275°F.

16. Once the pork shoulder has reached 203°F (about 2-3 hours wrapped) it is time to take off the pit and let rest so the juices can redistribute.

17. Rest for 30-45 minutes.

18. Now is the moment of truth. Try to pull out the bone and if it gives little to no resistance then your pork shoulder is cooked to perfection!

19. Shred it and serve between a bun with a little coleslaw on top. Enjoy!

Hoppin' John

Cooking Time: 15 Min

Ingredients:

- 2 Tbsp. Olive oil
- ½ C. onion, diced
- ¾ C. bell pepper, diced
- 15 oz. can black-eyed peas
- Salt and pepper, to taste
- ¼ lb. smoked pulled pork
- Chipotle peppers
- 2 C. cooked white rice
- Andouille sausage

Directions:

1. Pre-heat grill to 350°F and place a 10" cast iron skillet on grill and heat until very hot. 2. Place sausages on the grill and allow to cook for 8-10 minutes, turning once or twice, until cooked through. 3. Pour 2 Tbsp. olive oil into hot skillet and add onion, bell pepper and black-eyed peas. 4. Season with salt and pepper and allow to cook for 1-2 minutes, stirring occasionally. 5. Add smoked

pulled pork and Chipotle peppers and stir. 6. Add cooked rice to mixture. Close lid and allow to cook for 3-4 minutes. 7. Add grilled andouille sausage from Step

2. Remove from grill and serve. Enjoy!

Bbq Burnt Ends

Cooking Time: 4.5 Hrs

Ingredients:

- 5-8lbs pork belly
- 1 - 1.5 C. BBQ sauce
- Favorite pork rub
- 1 stick of butter
- 1/3 C. of rum
- 1/3 C. brown sugar

Directions:

1. Trim top layer of fat
2. Cut into 2" wide vertical strips
3. Rotate and cut again to create 2" squares
4. Place in aluminum pan and season well with your favorite pork rub
5. Mix squares to thoroughly cover with rub
6. Heat grill to 250°F
7. Space out cubes evenly within grill
8. Let smoke for 3 hours at 250°F
9. Remove from grill and place in pan
10. Add 1.5 C. of your favorite BBQ sauce
11. Add 1/3 C. rum, 1/3 C. brown sugar, and 1 stick of butter
12. Mix well to evenly cover cubes
13. Smoke for another 1.5 - 1.75 hours

Flavor Pro Quick And Easy Grilled Pork Tenderloin

Ingredients:

- 2 Pork Tenderloin
- 2 tsp Paprika
- 1 tsp Garlic Powder
- 1 tsp Cilantro
- 1 tsp Oregano
- Salt and Pepper to Taste
- Olive Oil

Directions:

1. Blend spices together in a bowl. Rub pork with olive oil and then season liberally on both sides with spice blend.
2. Set up the Flavor Pro for direct cooking. Ignite burners and turn to medium high.
3. Place pork on the grill and cook for 8 to 10 minutes per side or until the internal temperature reads 165 degrees.
4. Remove from grill and let rest for 10 minutes.

St. Louis-style Ribs

Cooking Time: 5 Hrs

Ingredients:

- 3 racks of ribs
- Ribs BBQ rub, to taste
- 1 can Coca-Cola
- 1 C. molasses
- ½ C. agave nectar
- ½ C. Jack Daniels Tennessee whiskey (or a good bourbon whiskey)
- ½ C. apple cider vinegar
- ¼ C. honey, and more as needed for wrapping ribs
- 1 Tbsp. cayenne pepper
- Apple juice
- Brown sugar
- 12 oz. bottle of squeeze butter

Directions:

1. Rinse rib racks and pat dry with paper towel. Remove membrane from each rack by carefully

prying back using the back of a sharp knife. Discard membrane. Flip racks and trim loose ends and excess fat.Tip: Use a paper towel to help hold the membrane, as it's slippery.

2. Season ribs generously with Ribs BBQ Rub, or your favorite rub.

3. When setting up the grill, use a full chimney of unlit charcoal in the attached Side Fire Box and pour another ½ chimney of hot coals on top to ensure good smoke and a temperature of 275°F. Add Applewood chunks on top.

4. Adjust the charcoal grate to the highest setting in the main compartment. Place an aluminum pan on the grate and fill halfway with apple juice. Smoke ribs for 1 hour and mist with apple juice. Close lid and smoke for another 3 hours. 5. After 3 hours, remove ribs from grill and wrap. Before wrapping, spread a layer of brown sugar, butter and honey onto aluminum foil. Place ribs meat side down and wrap securely. 6. Transfer wrapped ribs to the grill and smoke at 275°F for another hour. 7. During the last 10-20 minutes of smoking the ribs, make the glaze. Combine 1 can of Coca-Cola, molasses, agave nectar, whiskey, apple cider vinegar, honey and cayenne pepper in a saucepan and bring to a boil, stirring occasionally. Reduce heat to a simmer until glaze is thickened.

5. Remove ribs from the grill and carefully drain juices before brushing with glaze, slicing and serving.

Flat Iron Griddle Breakfast Sandwich

Cooking Time: 5 Min

Ingredients:

- 2 Cups Of Kodiak Cakes Pancake And Waffle Mix
- 2 Cups Of Water
- 6 Eggs
- Egg Rings
- Syrup
- 1 Pack Of Bacon

Directions:

1. Mix pancake and waffle mix with water until the mix is no longer lumpy. Place egg rings on griddle and pour pancake batter into the egg rings , add a little swirl of syrup while batter is cooking. Once the batter has a nice bubble to it remove the egg ring and flip the griddle cake. Scramble or fry your eggs and cook the bacon , construct sandwich and enjoy

Breakfast Bomb - Homemade Stuffed Breakfast Sausage

Ingredients:

- Pork Sausage - 1 Lb
- 5 Eggs
- Bacon - 2 Strips
- Hash Browns - 1/4 Cup
- Shredded Cheese
- Salt & Pepper to Taste

Directions:

1. BBQ Fiends created what we think sounds like one of the best breakfasts ever. Instead of the standard, sausage with your breakfast, he filled the sausage with all of the other breakfast ingredients.

2. These sausages are stuffed with hash browns, eggs and cheese so you'll definitely stay full all day!

3. Begin by pre-heat the grill to 325 F.

4. As the grill is getting up to temp start to create the filling for the sausage. Scramble your eggs and add salt and pepper to taste.

5. Cook bacon and hash-browns to preference. Combine all ingredients together to use for the filling.Tip: Remove the eggs from the heat before they are completely finished, as they will finish once they are on the grill.

6. Lay the pork sausage out flat in a rectangle shape making sure it is evenly spread out. Place your filling in the middle and add cheese on top if desired.Tip: Remember that the sausage has to close around the filling so if needed remove some of the filling to help with closing and shaping the sausage into a log shape.

7. Bring all edges of the sausage to the top to enclose the filling. Ensure that the filling can no longer be seen and the sausage has completely enclosed it in a log shape.

8. Place on the grill at 325 F cooking on indirect heat.

9. Once the sausage is cooked and the internal temp reads 165 F it is time to pull. (This will be around the hour mark)

10. Cut the log into slices and serve with your favorite syrup!

Oktoberfest Schweinshaxe - Smoked Pork Shanks

Cooking Time: 10 Min

Ingredients:
- Pork Shanks
- 2 Tbsp White Peppercorns
- 2 Tsps Caraway Seeds
- 2 Tsp Kosher Salt
- 1 Tsp Garlic Powder
- 1 Tsp Baking Powder
- 1 Tsp Dried Thyme

Directions:
1. In a skillet, lightly toast the white peppercorns and carways just until they become fragrant (toast separately) Put toasted peppercorns and caraway seeds into a spice grind and coarsely grind In a separate bowl, mix peppercorns and caraway seeds and remaining dry ingredients Rinse and pat the pork shanks dry with a paper towel Score the skin about every 2 inches all the way around they shank. Make sure to cross hatch the skin. Lightly oil the shanks and season w/ the seasoning mix be careful to get some spices underneath the skin at the score marks Heat smoker to an ambient temperature of 250 degrees. If using wood as fuel, I recommend hickory as it works well with the flavor profile of the shanks Insert an internal meat probe into the thickest part of the shank Smoke until internal temperature is approximately 190 to 200 degrees Remove shanks and lightly tent with foil Heat grill to searing temperature - anywhere from 500 to 600 degrees Sear pork shank skin rotating every 3 to 5 minutes until skin is crispy Remove from grill and server immediately. Skin should be crispy and meat should be fork tender.

Flavor Pro Pork Steaks

Cooking Time: 12 Min

Ingredients:
- 4 Large Pork Steaks
- 1 Cup Stout Beer
- 2 Tbsp Canola Oil
- 3 Tbsp Minced Garlic
- 1/4 Cup Soy Sauce
- 2 Tbsp Worcestershire Sauce
- 1/3 Cup Packed Brown Sugar
- 2 tsp Hot Sauce

- 1 Tbsp Dijon Mustard
- 1 tsp Onion Powder
- 2 tsp Salt
- 2 tsp Pepper

Directions:

1. Add all ingredients to your favorite food-safe marinade container or ziplock bag along with the pork steaks.

2. Massage marinade into the steaks to ensure an even coating.

3. Store the container in the refrigerator for at least 2 hours but storing overnight is optimal.

4. Prepare the Flavor Pro for direct heat grilling (High, 400°F+) For best results, fill all three zones of the Flavor Drawer with charcoal and add a few wood chunks for added smoke flavor. Turn all four gas burners on high to ignite the coals, once the coals are fully lit, turn off the gas completely. Leave both smoke stacks fully open.

5. Remove pork steaks from the marinade and place them on the grill directly over the coals.

6. Cook for 4-6 minutes per side.

Grilled Stuffed Pork Chops

Cooking Time: 15 Min

Ingredients:
- 1" thick bone-in pork chops
- 1 Tbsp. unsalted butter
- 2 Tbsp. chopped almonds
- 4 C. baby spinach, finely chopped
- 4 oz. cream cheese
- ¼ Tsp. cayenne pepper
- ¼ Tsp. salt
- Original All-Purpose BBQ Rub, to taste

Directions:

1. Pre-heat grill to 375°F. Rinse the pork chops and pat dry with paper towel. Cut a deep pocket in the side of each chop with a small sharp knife, cutting toward the bone but not all the way through. 2. In a medium bowl, combine butter, chopped almonds, baby spinach, cream cheese, cayenne pepper and salt and mix well to make stuffing. 3. Transfer mixture to a piping bag without a tip, fill pork chops with mixture and secure with toothpicks. 4. Generously season both sides of each chop with Original All-Purpose BBQ rub, or your favorite rub, to taste. 5. Place stuffed pork chops on the grill over direct heat at 375°F for 6 minutes per side, turning halfway through for good sear marks. Move to indirect side of grill to finish cooking if needed.

2. Pork chops are done when internal temperature reaches 145°F. Remove from grill and set aside to rest for 5 minutes and remove toothpicks before serving. Enjoy!

Father's Day Baby Back Ribs

Cooking Time: 6 Hrs

Ingredients:
- 1 C. warmed honey
- 1/2 C. yellow or Dijon mustard
- 2 oz. brown sugar
- 1 oz smoked paprika
- 1 Tbsp. black pepper
- 1 Tsp. crushed red pepper flakes
- 2 C. water
- 2 oz chipotle peppers

Directions:

1. Mix mustard and honey in small bowl

2. Pour over ribs and coat evenly

3. Mix together brown sugar, black pepper, red pepper flakes, and paprika in a bowl

4. Coat ribs generously with the rub mix

5. Wrap in aluminum foil and leave in the refrigerator for 24 hours

6. Pre heat grill to 275° F

7. Mix 2 C. of water and 2 oz. of chipotle peppers in a cast iron skillet

8. Baste with liquid in skillet every hour

9. Smoke for about 6 hours or until internal temperature reaches 175° F

Quick And Easy Grilled Pork Tenderloin

Cooking Time: 25 Min

Ingredients:
- 1 Pork Tenderloin
- 1 Tsp Paprika
- 1/2 Tsp Garlic Powder
- 1/2 Tsp Cilantro
- 1/2 Tsp Oregano
- Salt and Pepper to Taste
- Olive Oil

Directions:

1. Blend spices together in a bowl. Rub pork with olive oil and then season liberally on both sides with spice blend. Set up the Flavor Pro™ for direct cooking. Ignite burners and turn to medium high. Place pork on the grill and cook for 8 to 10 minutes per side or until the internal temperature reads 165 degrees. Remove from grill and let rest for 10 minutes.

Grilled Pork And Sweet Potato Verde Chili

Cooking Time: 3.5 Hrs

Ingredients:
- 2 Lbs Pork
- 2 Large Sweet Potatoes - Diced
- 3 Ears of Corn on the Cob
- 1 Bunch Cilantro - Stems Cut from Leaves and Set Aside
- 2 Cloves of Garlic
- 3 Tbsp Ground Cumin
- 1/2 Cup olive Oil or Avocado Oil
- 2 Cups Salsa Verde
- 6 Cups Chicken Stock
- 1 Can White Beans
- Salt and Pepper to taste
- Garnish: Cilantro, Radish, Red Onion, and/or Sour Cream

Directions:

1. Remove stems from fresh cilantro, and add to blender with garlic cloves, oil, cumin, and a pinch of s&p. Pulse until smooth and combined.

2. Preheat Char-Griller to high heat, I recommend charcoal for this recipe as it will add even more flavor.

3. In a large bowl, transfer corn, pork, and sweet potato pieces. Pour blended marinade over the ingredients and toss to combine. Once grill is heated, add all to grill, and cook until charred on each side, 6-8 mins per side. Remove and set aside.

4. Once the grilled items are cool to the touch, dice sweet potatoes and pork into similar sized pieces, and cut corn off the cob. Transfer these items to a soup pot, adding salsa verde, & chicken stock. Bring to a simmer over low.

5. Add ½ cup chopped cilantro leaves, the white beans, and S&P to taste. Simmer on low partially covered for 3 hours, until pork is fall apart tender, and chili has thickened. Serve with garnishes of choice and enjoy! Leftover Chili can stay in the fridge for up to 7 days, and frozen for 6 months.

Orange Pork Belly Burnt Ends

Cooking Time: 4 Hrs

Ingredients:

- Pork Belly (2-3 Lbs)
- 1 Tsp Kosher Salt
- 1/2 Tsp Coarse Black Pepper
- 1/2 Tsp Garlic Powder
- 1 Disposable Aluminum Pan
- 1/2 Cup Orange Juice (For Spritzing)
- Hickory Wood (Splits or Chunks)
- 1/2 Cup White Sugar
- 1 Tbsp Soy Sauce
- 2 Tbsp Rice Vinegar
- 1 Tsp Sesame Oil
- 1/4 Tsp Ginger Powder
- 1/4 Tsp Garlic Powder
- 1/2 Tsp Red Chili Flakes

Directions:

1. Cut the pork belly into 1-1 ½ inch cubes. Combine salt, pepper, and garlic powder in a small bowl and season the pork belly cubes on all sides. Whisk together all the orange sauce ingredients in a medium size bowl and place in the refrigerator for later use.

2. Heat your smoker to a temperature of 275 F. Place the pork belly cubes into the side of the smoker that is furthest away from the fire. Spritz every 40-45 minutes until the pork belly starts to read an internal temp between 190 F – 200 F. *Tip* Place a water pan inside the smoker next to the fire box to help with added moisture.

3. Place the pork belly cubes in an aluminum pan and add the orange sauce mixture. Return the pan into the smoker maintaining 275 F.

4. Once the orange sauce has reduced and the cubes look caramelized it is time to pull from the smoker (This should take approximately 25-35 minutes). Top with sesame seeds and green onions. Enjoy!

Oktoberfest Schweinebraten

Cooking Time: 30-40 Min

Ingredients:

- Boneless Pork Shoulder With Fat Cap and Skin
- 4-6 Cups Of Vegetable Broth
- 4 Carrots
- 4 Leeks
- 4 Celery Stalks
- 4 Medium Sized Onions
- 2 Bottles Of German Beer
- Salt & Pepper To Taste
- 3 Tbsp Butter

Directions:

1. Lay shoulder fat side down in a roasting pan Pour in enough vegetable broth to keep the fat cap covered Place on the grill at 300F for 30-40 minutes. This will help soften the skin. Cut up your vegetables into 1-2" lengths. Cut the onions into chunks Remove the meat from grill and set aside for next step Butter up your roasting pan and fill with your cut up vegetables. Brown the vegetables slightly Cut 1/2" or 1cm cubes into the fat cap being careful not to cut into the meat. Season with salt and pepper and get it down into the cube crevices. Pour the vegetable broth on top of your browned vegetables not too much, just enough to cover them. Place your seasoned shoulder on top of the vegetable bed Pour 2 bottles of your favorite dark german beer over shoulder and vegetables Raise grill heat to 340-350F and cook until internal temp of 160-165F checking throughout. Cut up and enjoy!

Smoked Chili Hotdogs

Cooking Time: 20-30 Min

Ingredients:

- 8 hotdogs
- 8 hotdog buns
- 8 slices of cheese
- 1 cup of shredded cheese
- 1 can chili sauce
- 4 Tbsp. butter
- 1/2 Tsp. granulated garlic

Directions:

1. Place hotdog buns (whole) in a greased 9x13 pan
2. Cut hotdog sized slots with a knife
3. With finger, pack cut part of bun down
4. Melt butter and garlic
5. Baste buns with the butter and garlic mixture
6. Place a slice of cheese into each bun
7. Add some chili
8. Place the hotdog on top of the chili
9. Add more chili
10. Top with shredded cheese
11. Sprinkle with parsley flakes
12. Place on smoker at 250°F
13. Smoke for 20-30 minutes or until cheese is melted

Bacon Wrapped Kielbasa Bites

Cooking Time: 50 Min

Ingredients:

- 14 oz Kielbasa
- 12 oz bacon
- 8 oz BBQ sauce
- Fresh or dry parsley
- Your Favorite Rub

Directions:

1. Pre-heat grill to 350°
2. Slice kielbasa into 1" pieces or same size as the bacon strip.
3. Wrap bacon around the kielbasa.
4. Lightly coat the kielbasa bacon wrapped bites with Char-Griller Original Rub or your favorite rub.
5. Place the kielbasa bacon wrapped bites on your baking rack. Tip: spray rack with olive or vegetable spray to avoid sticking.
6. Next, put the baking rack with the kielbasa bacon bites in your grill at 350°F.
7. After 30 minutes or when bacon becomes golden brown begin to glaze the kielbasa bacon wrapped bites with bbq sauce to your liking.
8. Stick the kielbasa bacon wrapped bites with toothpicks for easy removal and easy handling to eat. Remove them from the grill.
9. Place in a serving tray or if tailgating, eat them right off the grill. Tip: serve with BBQ sauce on the side for dipping.
10. Enjoy!

Certified Pork Butt

Cooking Time: 12-20 Hrs

Ingredients:

- 2 Pork butts (6-10 lbs. each)
- Apple juice
- Your favorite rub/seasoning
- Mustard

Directions:

1. Remove the pork butt from the plastic wrap & pat dry using a paper towel.
2. Tip: Choose a pork butt with a full fat cap. This helps the meat while it's smoking for a long period of time.

3. Trim the excess fat that is loose and pulls up easily. Score the fat cap 1/8 to 1/4-inch-deep diagonally, spaced out 1/2 to 1 inch apart.

4. Tip: Scoring the meat allows the seasoning and smoke to penetrate into the pork butt.

5. Fill the marinade injector with apple juice and inject into the top and sides of the meat.

6. Spread a coating of mustard using a basting brush all over the pork butt.

7. Tip: This allows the rub to stick to the pork butt.

8. Generously season the pork butt on all sides with your favorite rub.

9. Tip: After seasoning, wrap in Saran Wrap and store in refrigerator overnight or 8-10 hours. This allows the rubs to penetrate and apple juice to tenderizer the pork butt.

10. Chef's Note: I used a combination of the Char-Griller Original All-Purpose BBQ Rub, Char-Griller Ribs BBQ Rub, TexJoy Butt & Rib Tickler Pork Rub, Barker BBQ All Purpose House Blend Rub and Southside Market Barbecue Oak Smoked Black Pepper, Coarse Ground

11. Cooking Directions

12. Ignite charcoal and preheat smoker to 225°F.

13. Add boiling water to the drip pan and place under grill grate.

14. Tip: This will add moisture for the cook and collect the drippings .

15. Smoke the pork butts f or 2 hours per pound at 225°F, until the meat reaches an internal temperature of 160°F.

16. Tip: Maintain a 225°F temperature, check fire hourly or when needed. Also spritz with apple juice every time you add fuel to your fire. Spritzing adds moisture and flavor. It prevents the pork butt from drying out and helps to create the bark. Monitor the temperature using a folding probe thermometer and/or remote thermometer.

17. Chef's Note: I used Fogo Eucalyptus Lump Charcoal for the heat and Mesquite mini logs for the smoke. Always keep the smoke stack vent open to allow the smoke to flow over the meat. Maintain the heat of smoker by adjusting the side vent on the fire box. Slightly close it if your fire gets too hot.

18. Remove the pork butts from the smoker and double wrap in foil. Before closing the wrap, add 1 C. apple juice and 1 stick of butter for each pork butt, more seasoning and BBQ sauce, to taste.

19. Place back in smoker and cook until the pork butt reaches an internal temperature of 199°F, then remove from the smoker.

20. Tip: Wrap pork butt in a large towel and place in a cooler or just set to the side for a minimum of 1-2 hours for resting. This allows the meat to cook down and stop cooking and is a major key in the process.

21. After resting, remove the towel and foil. Pull apart the pork using two forks or meat claws.

22. Make pulled pork sandwiches and endless pulled pork dishes. Enjoy!

Ultimate Pork Belly Sliders

Cooking Time: 2:15 Hrs

Ingredients:

- 4 lb. pork belly
- Yellow mustard
- Original All-Purpose BBQ rub, to taste
- Your favorite sweet BBQ rub, to taste
- Hawaiian sweet rolls or your favorite roll for sliders

- Your favorite toppings
- Your favorite BBQ sauce

Directions:

1. Remove the skin from the pork belly and season the top generously with a layer of yellow mustard, followed by Original All-Purpose BBQ rub and your favorite sweet BBQ sauce, to taste.
2. Pre-heat grill to 275°F for indirect heat with a Smokin' Stone. Allow the belly to smoke for 2 hours or until internal temperature reaches 175°F. Remove the belly from the grill and allow to rest.
3. After removing the pork belly and Smokin' Stone, stir the charcoal and open up both vents to allow the grill to reach maximum temperature for searing.
4. While the grill is heating up, slice the pork belly into ¼" thick strips and arrange on the grill. Work in batches if needed. Fry the belly for 3 minutes on each side, to allow the fat to render. Season the belly with BBQ rub again, if desired.
5. Slice the pack of Hawaiian sweet rolls in half and arrange the pork belly on the bottom half. Cover with the top half and brush with melted butter and garlic, if desired. Place the rolls in a large pan and back onto the grill to crisp up for 10 minutes.
6. Remove the pan from the grill and allow the rolls to cool slightly before slicing into individual sliders. Add your favorite toppings and sauce and enjoy!

Baby Back Ribs

Cooking Time: 3 Hrs

Ingredients:

- Salt
- Pepper
- Brown Sugar
- Garlic Salt
- Onion Salt
- Paprika

Directions:

1. Mix everything together and rub on ribs
2. Cover the ribs with foil and refrigerate overnight
3. Grill on 250° for 3 hours and take off
4. Throw your favorite BBQ sauce on and refold and grill till the BBQ sauce caramelizes. Take off and enjoy!

DESSERTS

Salted Caramel Chocolate Tart

Cooking Time: 20 Min

Ingredients:

- 1- 8 oz Bag of Sea Salt Kettle Potato Chips, Crushed (Crust)
- 1/4 Cup Flour (Crust)
- 5 Tbsp Unsalted Butter, Melted (Crust)
- 1 Cup Sugar (Caramel)
- 1/2 Cup Heavy Cream (Caramel)
- 6 Tbsp Unsalted Butter (Caramel)
- 1 tsp Sea Salt (Caramel)
- 10 Oz Semisweet Chocolate Chips (Chocolate Layer)
- 1/4 Cup Heavy Cream (Chocolate Layer)
- 1/4 Cup Sugar (Chocolate Layer)
- 2 tsp Vanilla Extract (Chocolate Layer)
- 2 Large Eggs (Chocolate Layer)

Directions:

1. Light grill for indirect heat and heat to 350.
2. In a large bowl, combine crushed chips, melted butter, and flour. Mix until combined.
3. Press into tart pan and place on grill. Bake for 15 minutes.
4. Remove from grill and allow to cool.
5. In a sauce pan over medium heat, add sugar and allow to melt completely, stirring frequently.
6. Add cream and butter, stir until combined.
7. Add sea salt and allow to boil for 5 minutes.
8. Remove from heat and allow to cool for 15 minutes.
9. Pour caramel onto crust.
10. In a saucepan over medium heat, add cream and allow to heat up.
11. Add chocolate chips and sugar, stir until melted and smooth.
12. Add eggs one at a time stirring until combined.
13. Add vanilla and stir.
14. Pour chocolate until crust.
15. Place tart on grill and allow to bake for 20 minutes.
16. Remove from grill and let cool.

Grilled S'mores 4 Ways

Servings: 4

Cooking Time: 5 Min

Ingredients:

- Graham Crackers - 4 Full Crackers
- Large Marshmallows - 4
- Milk Chocolate Bar
- Dark Chocolate Bar
- Cookie Butter
- Peanut and Caramel Candy Bar
- Chili Powder
- Peanut Butter

Directions:

1. Heat grill to 350 degrees
2. Break four graham crackers in half and lay out.
3. Top the first graham cracker with milk chocolate bar and peanut butter.
4. Top the second graham cracker with milk chocolate and cookie butter
5. Top third graham cracker with dark chocolate and a sprinkle of chili powder.
6. Top fourth graham cracker with Snickers Bar cut in half longways.
7. Top each graham cracker with a marshmallow and the other half of the graham cracker.
8. Wrap each s'mores in its own foil packet.
9. Place on warming rack of the grill for 4 to 5 minutes.
10. Enjoy.

Bourbon Glaze For Candied Bacon Scones

Cooking Time: 15 Min

Ingredients:

- Bourbon - 3 Tbsp
- Vanilla - 1 tsp
- Powdered Sugar - 2 cups
- Milk - 4 Tbsp

Directions:

1. Place all ingredients in a small pan and stir to combine. Place pan on grill and allow to heat through for 15 minutes. Stir half way through. Remove from grill and cool. Open grill vents and increase temperature to 400 to cook the scones. Make the scone dough.

Grilled Stuffed Peaches

Cooking Time: 20 Min

Ingredients:

- 1- 2 peaches per person
- 2 Tbsp. honey, divided
- 4 oz. blue cheese, or to taste
- Coarse black pepper, to taste
- 2-3 slices of bacon, for garnish

Directions:

1. Rinse peaches and dry with paper towel. Slice in half, remove stone and cut the pit hole slightly larger.

2. Fry bacon in a pan to desired crispness according to package directions, drain grease and crumble when cool. Set aside in a small bowl.

3. Place peaches cut side down directly on the grill at 350°F for 5-7 minutes, depending on the size.

4. Turn peaches over and fill holes with blue cheese and crumbled bacon and bake for 5-7 minutes, until peaches are softened and cheese is melted.

5. Remove peaches from grill, drizzle with honey and sprinkle with coarse black pepper to serve.

Chocolate Chip Skillet Cookie

Cooking Time: 25-30 Min

Ingredients:

- 2 C. all-purpose flour
- 1 C. butter, melted
- 1 C. brown sugar
- ½ C. sugar
- 2 eggs, beaten
- 1 Tsp. vanilla extract
- 1 Tsp. baking soda
- ½ Tsp. salt
- ¾ C. milk chocolate chunks
- ¾ C. semi-sweet chocolate chips

Directions:

1. Pre-heat grill to 325°F. In a large bowl, combine melted butter and add sugars, stirring until dissolved. 2. Add eggs and vanilla and mix well. 3. Stir in flour, baking soda, and salt. Add in chocolate and stir to combine. 4. Transfer dough into heated cast iron skillet and spread evenly. 5. Bake at 325°F for 25-30 minutes or until the edges are golden brown. The inside will still be slightly gooey.

2. To serve, top with ice cream and eat warm.

Plum Galette

Cooking Time: 45-50 Min

Ingredients:

- 1½ C. and 3 Tbsp. all-purpose flour
- 1 ½ sticks unsalted butter, cut into ½" pieces
- ¼ Tsp. salt

- 1/3 C. ice water
- ¼ C. plus 1/3 C. sugar, reserve 1 Tsp.
- 3 Tbsp. ground almonds
- 2½ lbs. large plums, halved, pitted and cut into ½" wedges
- ½ C. good-quality plum preserves, strained if chunky or seedy
- Corn meal, for dusting

Directions:

1. Put 1½ C. flour, butter and salt into a food processor and mix for 5 seconds. 2. Add ice water and mix for 5 seconds longer, just until the dough holds together. Small pieces of butter should still be visible. 3. Remove the dough and gather it into a ball. On a lightly floured surface, roll out the dough into a large circle, 1/8" thick. 4. Drape the dough over the rolling pin and transfer to a large baking sheet. Refrigerate the dough until firm, 10-20 minutes. 5. While dough is chilling, pre-heat grill to 400°. In a small bowl, combine ¼ C. of the sugar with the ground almonds and 3 Tbsp. flour and mix well. Spread evenly over the dough to within 2" of the edge. 6. Arrange plum wedges on top and dot with butter. Sprinkle 1/3 C. sugar over the fruit. Fold the edge of the dough up over the plums to create a 2" border.

2. Tip: If the dough feels cold and firm when folding up the edges, wait a few minutes until it softens to prevent cracking.

3. Sprinkle the border with the remaining 1 Tsp. sugar. 7. Transfer the galette to a pre-heated pizza stone dusted with corn meal to prevent sticking, and bake at 400°F for 45-50 minutes, until the fruit is very soft and the crust is golden brown. 8. Remove from the grill and evenly brush the preserves over the hot fruit.

4. Allow the galette to cool before slicing and serving. Enjoy!

Glazed Oatmeal Raisin Cookies

Cooking Time: 15 Min

Ingredients:
- 2 C. oats
- 2 C. all-purpose flour
- 1 Tbsp. baking powder
- 2 Tsp. cinnamon
- ½ Tsp. nutmeg
- 1 Tsp. salt
- 2 sticks unsalted butter, softened
- 1 C. sugar
- ½ C. brown sugar
- 2 eggs
- ½ C. raisins
- 1 C. powdered sugar
- 1 Tbsp. vanilla extract
- 2-3 Tbsp. milk

Directions:

1. Pre-heat grill to 350°F. 2. In a medium bowl combine the oats, flour, baking powder, cinnamon, nutmeg, and salt. Mix well and set aside. 3. In a large bowl whisk the butter, sugar, and brown sugar together until sugar is dissolved. Add in the eggs one at a time, stirring well until combined. 4. Add the oat mixture to the butter mixture and stir until combined. Fold in the raisins. 5. Drop 1 Tbsp. of cookie batter onto cookie sheets, 2" apart. Bake 15 minutes or until the edges are golden brown. Remove from grill and transfer to a wire rack to cool. 6. While cookies are cooling, prepare icing by combining the powdered sugar and vanilla in a bowl. Gradually add in milk until mixture is thick but spreadable.

2. Dunk the top of each cookie into the icing and let the excess drip off. Serve warm.

Candied Bacon Scones With Bourbon Glaze

Cooking Time: 15 Min

Ingredients:

- All Purpose Flour - 3 Cups
- Salt - 3/4 tsp
- Baking Powder - 1 Tbsp
- Sugar - 1/3 cup
- Cinnamon - 1/2 tsp
- Vanilla Extract - 1.5 tsp
- Heavy Cream - 1.5 Cups
- Chopped Bacon - 1/3 cup
- Heavy Cream - 1/4 cup

Directions:

1. Look here for the Candied Bacon Recipe and here for the Bourbon Glaze Recipe.

2. Have the Candied Bacon and Bourbon Glaze Ready nearby. Whisk together flour, salt, baking powder, sugar, and cinnamon. Add 1 1/2 c. cream, vanilla, candied bacon, and stir to combine. Divide dough in half. Flour a cutting board and pat each half into a 6" circle. Brush each circle of dough with the remaining cream. Place dough on parchment paper and cut into 6 triangles. Pull each wedge apart slightly and place in the freezer for 10 minutes. Transfer scones on the parchment paper to the grill grates. Bake for 15 minutes or until golden brown. Remove from grill and allow to cool. Using a 1/4 measuring cup, pour glaze over each scone and top with remaining chopped bacon.

Grilled Pumpkin Pie With Smoked Gingersnap Crust

Cooking Time: 45 To 60 Min

Ingredients:

- 15 Gingersnaps
- 5 Whole Graham Crackers, Broken Apart
- 2 Tbsp Light Brown Sugar
- 4 Tbsp Unsalted Butter, Melted
- 1 - 15 oz Can Pumpkin Puree
- 1 - 14 oz Can of Sweetened Condensed Milk
- 1 Tsp Cinnamon
- 1/2 tsp Ground Ginger
- 1/2 tsp Nutmeg
- 1/2 tsp Ground Cloves
- 2 Eggs, Lightly Beaten

Directions:

1. Add charcoal and a handful of mesquite wood chips to AKORN. Add the Smokin' Stone and preheat to 350 degrees F.

2. Place metal tin of gingersnaps and graham crackers on the grill.

3. Allow the cookies to smoke for 15 minutes.

4. Combine gingersnaps, brown sugar and butter into a food processor and process to moist crumbs.

5. Spoon crumbs into a greased pie pan and press into pan to form crust.

6. Return pie pan to grill and cook for 10 minutes.

7. Remove and allow to cool for 10 minutes.

8. While crust is cooling, whisk together pumpkin, sweetened condensed milk, eggs, and spices until combined.

9. Pour mixture into crust.

10. If desired, place foil around edges of crust to protect it from burning.

11. Return pie to grill and cook for an hour or until a toothpick inserted in the center comes out clean.

12. Cool and serve with whipped cream.

Candy Jar Brownies

Cooking Time: 25 Min

Ingredients:

- 20 Tablespoons Butter (Unsalted)
- 2 Cups White Sugar
- 1 Teaspoon Vanilla
- Four Large Eggs
- 1.5 Cups Unsweetened Cocoa Powder
- 1 Cup All Purpose Flour
- 2 Tablespoons Espresso Powder
- One Tablespoon Salt
- Variety of Candy (About 3 Cups)

Directions:

1. We didn't stop there. We also decided to cook it on the Char-Griller AKORN Kamado Grill because it is so versatile. The chocolate smell plus charcoal...we were in heaven. Before you start, check out our Guide to Baking on the AKORN.
2. Preheat AKORN to 350°F.
3. Cut up a variety of candy bars. Place in individual bowls.
4. Unwrap candy pieces that have foil and add those to individual bowls.
5. In a large bowl, cream together butter and sugar with hand mixer. Mix for 3 minutes.
6. To creamed butter and sugar, add vanilla and eggs. Mix together.
7. Sift four and cocoa into the bowl with the wet ingredients.
8. Add espresso powder and salt. Mix everything together.
9. Note: This mixture will be extremely thick. This is okay. The chocolate from the candy will melt, adding extra moisture to the brownie.
10. Butter baking pan. We used a foil pan so it wouldn't get smoke stains, but any 11 by 9 pan will do.
11. Add 1/3 of the brownie mixture to the bottom of the pan. Spread evenly.
12. Add 1/3 of the candy. (We used the Lava Cake Hersey Kisses and Heath Bar Pieces).
13. Add the second third of the brownie batter. Spread as evenly as you can.
14. Add the second third of the candy. (We used Hersey Cookie Bar and Butterfinger pieces)
15. Add the final layer of brownie batter. Spread evenly.
16. Add the final pieces if candy to decorate the top. (We used Reeses Hearts and M&Ms).
17. Bake on the AKORN for 20 to 25 minutes. Use a toothpick to test if it is done.
18. Cool, cut into pieces and enjoy!
19. Note: Use both the vents to adjust the temperature on the AKRON. More closed vents will help it cool down, open vents will help it heat up. Airflow is key.

Smoked Candied Pecans

Cooking Time: 1 Hrs

Ingredients:

- 1 Lb Pecan Halves
- 3/4 Cup White Sugar
- 1 tsp Ground Cinnamon
- Pinch of Salt
- Pinch of Nutmeg
- 1 Egg White
- 1 Tbsp Water

Directions:

1. Pre-heat Char-Griller smoker to 250 F.
2. In a large bowl whisk together egg white and water until frothy. In a separate bowl combine

sugar, ground cinnamon, salt, and nutmeg. Stir until well mixed.

3. Add pecan halves to bowl with the egg white mixture and toss until well coated. Add sugar mixture to the pecans and toss until evenly coated.

4. Place pecans evenly on a baking sheet and smoke at 250 F for one hour or until pecans are evenly browned. Enjoy!

Crème Brûlée

Cooking Time: 30-40 Min

Ingredients:

- 2 C. heavy cream
- 1 Tsp. vanilla extract
- ⅛ Tsp. salt
- 5 egg yolks
- ½ C. sugar, plus more for topping

Directions:

1. Pre-heat grill to 325°F. In a saucepan, combine cream, vanilla extract and salt and cook over low heat just until hot, stirring continuously. Remove from heat and set aside.

2. In a bowl, beat yolks and sugar together until well combined. Add a ¼ C. of the vanilla-cream mixture from Step 1 and stir to incorporate.

3. Pour sugar-egg mixture into remaining cream in saucepan and stir. Pour into four 6 oz. ramekins and place into a baking dish.

4. Fill dish with boiling water halfway up the sides of the ramekins. Bake at 325°F for 30-40 minutes, until centers are just set.

5. Remove from grill and sprinkle a thin layer of sugar on top of each custard.

6. Tip: Use a butane torch to gradually melt sugar until caramelized and golden brown on top.

Low Carb Blueberry Cobbler

Cooking Time: 45 Min

Ingredients:

- Fresh or Frozen Blueberries - 2 Cups
- Water - 1/4 Cup
- Lemon Juice - 1 Tablespoon
- Monkfruit Sweetener - 2 Tablespoons
- Stevia - 10 Drops
- Xanthan Gum - 1/8 Teaspoon
- Softened Butter Chopped into Pieces - 1/4 Cup
- Coconut Flour - 1/3 Cup
- Additional Monkfruit Sweetener - 1/3 Cup
- Ground Cinnamon - 1 Tablespoon

Directions:

1. In sauce pan add blueberries, water, lemon juice & sweetener. Bring to a light boil and add xanthan gum. Stir occasionally as it thickens. Then remove from heat.

2. For crumble topping, mix coconut flour, monkfruit & cinnamon. Combine well, then add butter. Mix with fingers until well incorporated & crumbly.

3. Pour blueberry sauce into cast iron skillet & top with cinnamon crumb topping. Bake on grill heated to 350° for about 30 mins or until it bubbles & topping browns.

Spooky Brain Cinnamon Buns

Cooking Time: 30 Min

Ingredients:

- One Can Cinnamon Rolls
- Strawberry Jam
- Cinnamon Roll Frosting

Directions:

1. Layer the dough in a pan up against each other in and shaped it to look like a brain.

2. Heat oven or grill to 350°

3. Bake the cinnamon rolls for 30 minutes

4. While the cinnamon buns are baking, add the strawberry fruit spread to the icing and mixed it.

5. Then add the icing on to the cinnamon buns when they are done baking.

Strawberry And Rhubarb Crumble Pie

Cooking Time: 35-40 Min

Ingredients:

- 1¼ C. and ¾ C. all-purpose flour, plus 2 Tbsp. for filling
- 1 C. unsalted butter, diced and divided
- 1 C. sugar
- ½ C. light brown sugar
- 1 large egg
- 2 C. fresh rhubarb, cut into ½" dice
- 2 C. fresh strawberries, stemmed and sliced
- ¼ Tsp. orange zest, finely grated, optional
- 2 Tbsp. cold water, or more as needed
- 1 Tsp. vanilla extract
- Cold water, as needed

Directions:

1. Add 1¼ C. flour and salt to a large bowl and cut in ½ C. of butter with a pastry blender until the mixture resembles coarse crumbs. 2. Gradually add cold water to crumb mixture, until dough holds together when pressed. 3. Shape into a ball and wrap in plastic. Refrigerate 30 minutes. 4. Turn dough onto a floured surface and roll into a circle large enough to cover a buttered pie dish. Place dough into pie dish, trim the edges and prick the bottom with a fork.

2. Crumble Topping

3. In a medium bowl, combine ¾ C. flour, light brown sugar, and remaining ½ C. of butter Mix using a pastry blender or electric mixer until it resembles coarse crumbs.

4. Filling:Pre-heat grill to 400°F. In a large bowl, whisk 2 Tbsp. flour, egg, 1 C. sugar and vanilla together, until sugar is dissolved. 2. Add strawberries and rhubarb and mix until just blended. Let stand for 30 minutes at room temperature. 3. After 30 minutes, pour filling into pie crust. Sprinkle crumble topping evenly over pie and cover loosely with foil. Bake at 400°F for 35-40 minutes or until filling is bubbly and crumble topping is golden brown. Remove foil during the last 10 minutes.

5. Cool on wire rack before slicing and serving.

Pineapple Upside-down Cake

Cooking Time: 45 Min

Ingredients:

- 20 oz. can pineapple slices in juice, drained, with juice reserved
- 6 oz. jar maraschino cherries without stems, drained
- 1 box yellow cake mix
- ¼ C. unsalted butter
- 1 C. brown sugar
- Vegetable oil, according to box directions
- Eggs, according to box directions

Directions:

1. Pre-heat grill to 350°F. Melt butter in a cast iron pan and sprinkle brown sugar evenly over butter.

2. Place pineapple slices in pan on top of brown sugar and place a cherry in the center of each pineapple slice. Add remaining cherries around slices.

3. Add enough water to reserved pineapple juice to measure 1 C. Make cake batter according to package directions, substituting pineapple juice mixture for water. Slowly pour batter over pineapple and cherries in an even layer.

4. Bake at 350°F for 45 minutes or until a toothpick inserted into the center comes out clean. Run a knife around the side of the pan to loosen cake. Place a serving plate upside down onto the pan and turn plate and pan over.

5. Allow topping to drizzle over cake, then remove pan and allow cake to cool before slicing. Store covered in refrigerator.

Akorn Cinnamon Streusel Coffee Cake

Cooking Time: 2 Hrs

Ingredients:

- 1 ½ cups all-purpose flour (Topping)
- 1 ¼ cups packed light-brown sugar (Topping)
- 1 ½ tsp ground cinnamon (Topping)
- 1 ½ sticks cold salted butter, cut into fifths (Topping)
- 1 ½ cups chopped toasted pecans (Topping)
- 1 tsp kosher salt (Topping)
- 1 ¼ tsp baking powder (Cake)
- ½ tsp baking soda (Cake)
- 1 stick salted butter (room temperature) (Cake)
- 2 cups all-purpose flour (Cake)
- 1 ¼ cup granulated sugar (Cake)
- ½ tsp kosher salt (Cake)
- 2 large eggs (Cake)
- 1 ½ tsp vanilla extract (Cake)
- 1 cup plain greek yogurt (Cake)
- 1 cup powdered sugar (Glaze)
- 2 tbsp milk (Cake)

Directions:

1. Oktoberfest doesn't have to be just brats and sauerkraut. Bryan Head, @thebbqhead, made a classic Cinnamon Streusel Coffee Cake recipe and used his AKORN to bake it!

2. Toast pecans. Preheat oven to 275°F. In a bowl, melt a half stick of salted butter and toss pecans in the butter. Lay out pecans evenly on a baking sheet and toast for one hour flipping every 15 minutes. Let cool. Chop coarsely and set aside. Make the streusel topping. Mix together flour, ¾ cup brown sugar, 1 tsp cinnamon, and 1 tsp of salt. Cut in butter with sturdy fork or rub in with your fingers until pea-sized clumps remain. Mix in ½ cup chopped pecans. Refrigerate until ready to use. Make the streusel center. Mix together remaining ½ cup brown sugar, ½ tsp cinnamon, and 1 cup pecans. Prepare AKORN for indirect heat at 325°F. Make your cake: Butter the pan. Use a 9-inch tube pan with a removable bottom for best results. Sift in flour, baking powder, baking soda, and ½ tsp salt into a mixing bowl. Beat butter and granulated sugar with a mixer on medium speed for 2 minutes. Beat in eggs, one at a time, then vanilla. Beat in flour mixture in 3 stages alternating with greek yogurt, beginning and ending with the flour. Continue to beat at medium speed until well combined. Add half the batter into the pan. Sprinkle on the streusel center mixture evenly. Add the rest of the batter and spread evenly using a spatula. Sprinkle on the streusel topping evenly over batter. Bake until cake shows golden brown and a toothpick inserted into the center comes out clean, about 1 hour. Transfer pan to a wire rack to cool. Remove cake from pan. Make the glaze: Mix together powdered sugar and milk until you get your desired consistency. Drizzle over cake and down the sides and middle. Slice and enjoy!

Cheesecake Stuffed Apples

Cooking Time: 60 Min

Ingredients:
- Medium Baking Apples (I used Pink Lady) - 4
- Softened Cream Cheese - 8 Ounces
- Egg - 1
- Sugar - 1/3 Cup
- Cinnamon - 1/4 Teaspoon
- Crushed Graham Crackers - 1/4 Cup
- Prepared Caramel Sauce for Garnish

Directions:
1. Light AKORN and heat to 325
2. Cut bottoms of apples just enough to make them stand up straight
3. Hollow out apples with an apple corer or melon baller. Leave a ¼ inch of flesh around sides and bottom
4. Mix cream cheese, egg, sugar, vanilla, and cinnamon together until smooth
5. Spoon cream cheese mixture into each apple, leaving 1/2 inch space at the top
6. Sprinkle tops with graham crackers
7. Place apples in a small aluminum pan and place on grill
8. Allow to bake for 50-60 minutes. Filling should look semi set and apples should be soft
9. Allow to cool at room temperature then place in refrigerator until cold
10. Before serving, drizzle with caramel sauce

Smoked Chocolate Chip Cookies

Cooking Time: 15 To 20 Min

Ingredients:
- 2.25 Cups All Purpose Flour
- 2 Sticks of Butter
- 1 tsp Salt
- 1/2 Cup Sugar
- 1 Cup Light Brown Sugar
- 3 tsp Baking Powder
- 2 Eggs
- 1 tsp Vanilla Extract
- 2 Tbsp Milk
- Chocolate Chips (Your Choice with How Much)
- Chopped Pecans (Your Choice How Much)

Directions:
1. Melt the butter in a small pan.
2. Sift the flour, salt, & baking powder into a bowl.
3. Pour the butter in a mixing bowl & cream with the white & brown sugars.
4. Add the eggs, milk, and vanilla to the creamed sugar & mix.
5. Slowly add the flour mixture to the wet ingredients, beating constantly.
6. Mix in the chocolate chips & pecans.
7. Place the cookie dough in the fridge for a minimum of 30 minutes.
8. Heat your Char-griller Smoker/Grill to 350° or you can bake them in an oven at the same temperature.
9. Using a spoon make the cookies into a ball shape and place on pizza stone or cookie sheet using parchment paper or peach butcher paper.
10. Place in smoker/grill and smoke for 15-20 minutes or until golden brown.
11. Remove the cookies from the smoker/grill and allow them to cool for 10 minutes.
12. Enjoy.

Puffy Pancake With Fruit Compote

Cooking Time: 15 Min

Ingredients:

- 4 large eggs
- 1 C. all-purpose flour
- 1 C. milk
- 2 Tbsp. granulated sugar
- ¼ Tsp. salt
- 2 Tbsp. butter
- 2 ripe bananas, peeled and sliced
- 1 pint blueberries
- 1 Tbsp. granulated sugar
- 1 Tbsp. lemon juice
- Confectioners' sugar

Directions:

1. Pre-heat grill to 425ºF, place a 10" cast iron skillet on grill and heat until very hot.

2. In a blender at medium speed, blend eggs, milk, flour, sugar, and salt together until smooth.

3. Remove skillet from the grill, add butter and swirl until melted. Pour batter into hot skillet and bake for 15 minutes until puffy and golden brown on the edges.

4. In a large bowl, toss bananas and blueberries with sugar and lemon juice to make compote.

5. Spoon compote onto pancake and sprinkle with confectioner's sugar. To serve, cut into wedges.

Lou's Peach Cobbler

Cooking Time: 50 Min

Ingredients:

- 5 large peaches, peeled, pitted and sliced
- 1 C. and 3 Tbsp. all-purpose flour
- ¼ C. brown sugar
- 1 C. sugar
- 1 Tsp. baking powder
- 1 Tsp. lemon juice
- ½ Tsp. grated lemon peel
- ½ Tsp. ground cinnamon
- ¼ Tsp. salt
- ¼ Tsp. ground nutmeg
- 1 large egg, lightly beaten
- ½ C. butter, melted

Directions:

1. Pre-heat grill to 375°F. Combine brown sugar, 3 Tbsp. flour, lemon juice, grated lemon peel and cinnamon in a bowl and mix well. 2. Place sliced peaches in a large cast iron pot with a lid and sprinkle sugar mixture over top. Do not stir. 3. Transfer to grill and allow to cook at 375°F for 10 minutes. 4. While peaches are cooking, make the dough. Add 1 C. flour, sugar, baking powder, salt, nutmeg, egg and melted butter to a food processor, pulse to combine and mix well until a dough forms. 5. Remove peaches from grill, tear dough into medium to large pieces and place over top of peaches until covered. Replace lid and return to grill. 6. Bake at 375°F for 40 minutes.

2. To serve, scoop onto a plate and top with whipped cream or vanilla ice cream. Enjoy!

Deep Dish Apple Pie

Cooking Time: 40 Min

Ingredients:

- 8 medium tart apples, cored, peeled and sliced (makes 10 C.)
- 2 C. and 3 Tbsp. all-purpose flour
- ½ C. shortening
- 2 large eggs
- ¼ C. cold water
- 2 Tbsp. apple cider vinegar

- 1 Tsp. lemon juice
- ¼ C. sugar
- ¼ C. brown sugar
- 1 Tsp. ground cinnamon
- ½ Tsp. ground nutmeg
- 1 Tbsp. milk
- Unsalted butter, softened

Directions:

1. Pre-heat grill to 350°. Add 2 C. flour to a large bowl and cut in shortening. Mix until crumbly.

2. In a small bowl, whisk 1 egg, water and apple cider vinegar together and gradually add to crumb mixture, tossing with a fork until dough holds together when pressed.

3. Shape into a ball and wrap in plastic. Refrigerate 30 minutes or overnight, if desired.

4. Filling: In a large bowl, toss apples with lemon juice, sugars, remaining flour, cinnamon and nutmeg until evenly coated. Arrange in a single layer on a baking sheet. 2. Place pan onto grill and bake at 350°F with lid closed for 10-15 minutes, until apples release their juices. 3. While apples are baking, turn dough out onto a floured surface and roll into 2 circles large enough to cover a buttered pie dish with an overhang of at least 1". Place 1 dough into pie dish and prick the bottom with a fork. 5. Remove apples from grill and place evenly into prepared pie dish. Place the other pie dough on top of the apples and crimp the edges. 6. In a small bowl, whisk 1 egg together with milk to make egg wash and brush over pie. Cut slits in top. 7. Bake at 350°F for 40 minutes or until crust is golden brown. Remove from grill and run a knife around the side of the pan to loosen pie.

5. Cool on a wire rack and serve with ice cream, if desired. Enjoy!

Chocolate Lava Cake

Cooking Time: 15 Min

Ingredients:

- ½ C. all-purpose flour
- 1 stick unsalted butter
- 2 oz. bittersweet chocolate
- 2 oz. semisweet chocolate
- 1¼ C. powdered sugar
- 2 eggs and 3 egg yolks
- 1 Tsp. vanilla extract

Directions:

1. Pre-heat grill to 425°F. Spray four 6 oz. ramekins with baking spray and place on a baking sheet.

2. Melt the butter, bittersweet chocolate and semisweet chocolate together in a pan on medium heat, stirring constantly. Stir in the sugar until dissolved.

3. Whisk in the eggs and egg yolks, then add vanilla. Gradually stir in flour. Divide the mixture among the ramekins.

4. Bake until the sides are firm and the centers are soft, about 15 minutes. Let stand 1 minute.

5. To serve, plate each cake while warm and serve with vanilla ice cream.

Skillet Brownie On The Grill

Ingredients:

- Softened Butter- 2 Tablespoons
- Heavy Whipping Cream- 1 Tablespoon
- Large Egg- 1
- Erythritol Blend (or Sweeter of Your Choice)- 3 Tablespoons
- Cocoa Powder- 2.5 Tablespoons

- Almond Flour- 2.5 Tablespoons
- Pinch of Sea Salt

Directions:

1. Preheat the grill to 350°.

2. Mix together all of the ingredients until smooth and spread the batter in a greased mini cast iron skillet.

3. Place the skillet directly on the preheated grill grate, close the grill, and bake for 6 to 8 minutes—or just until set. Do not over bake in the grill, as the hot skillet will continue to bake the brownie as it sits.

4. Top with sugar free vanilla ice cream, sugar free chocolate syrup, and a sliced strawberry. Serve warm.

5. This serves one to two, but can be doubled or tripled for more servings. Bake each batch in its own mini skillet.

Smoked Apple Crumb Pie

Cooking Time: 75 Min

Ingredients:
- Frozen Pie Crust
- 1 Cup Flour
- 1/3 Cup White Sugar
- Lemon Juice - 1/2 Tbs
- Lemon Zest - 1/3 tsp
- Cinnamon - 1 tsp
- Nutmeg - 1/8 tsp
- Flour - 3 Tbs (Topping)
- 1/3 Cup White Sugar
- 1/2 Cup Packed Brown Sugar
- 1/2 Cup Oats
- Stick of Butter

Directions:

1. Add Smokin' Stone to AKORN, add chunks of Applewood, and preheat grill to 350 degrees.

2. Combine flour, sugar, brown sugar, oats and butter. Mix with fork to make topping.

3. Peel, core and slice apples into thin slices.

4. Toss apples with sugar, lemon juice and zest, cinnamon, nutmeg, and flour.

5. Layer apples in pie shell and pour juice over apples.

6. Put crumb topping on top of apples.

7. Bake for 1 hour and 15 minutes.

8. Serve warm with ice cream or whipped cream.

Smoked White Chocolate Christmas Candy

Cooking Time: 1 Hrs

Ingredients:
- 3 Cups Cheerios
- 3 Cups Corn Chex
- 3 Cups Peanut Butter Chex
- 1 Cup Butter Snaps Pretzels
- 1.5 Cups M&Ms
- 32 oz white Chocolate Chips

Directions:

1. Smoke white chocolate chips using your Char-Griller Offset charcoal smoker.

2. Add 6 lit charcoals to the far side of firebox along with a mild smoking wood chunk. Maple wood goes well with this recipe. Feel free to leave vents fully open.

3. You will need 2 foil baking pans. Fill pan number one with a layer of ice cubes. About ¼ of the way full. Add white chocolate chips to the second pan. Place pan with white chocolate on top of the pan with the ice.

4. Place stacked pans in cooking chamber of your smoker. Keep as far away from fire box side as possible.

5. Smoke for 30-45 minutes. For a milder smoke flavor try 30 minutes. To impart a stronger smoke flavor, try 45 minutes.

6. Melt white chocolate over heat source.

7. Add white chocolate to a large saucepan or keep in foil pan.

8. Over medium heat or lit coals, melt until white chocolate is a smooth consistency able to be drizzled. Be sure to stir often and do not over melt.

9. In a large mixing bowl or 2 foil pans, combine dry ingredients (cheerios, corn chex, peanut butter chex, pretzels, and m&m's) making sure to evenly distribute the ingredients.

10. Drizzle white chocolate on the dry mixture. Stir in making sure to coat all the mixture in the white chocolate.

11. Lay out on parchment paper or leave in foil pans as a nice thin layer to dry/cool for 1 hour.

12. Break into small to medium pieces and enjoy!

13. This stores well in the fridge and the freezer!

Smoked Blueberry Crisp

Cooking Time: 45 Min

Ingredients:

- Blueberries - 5 Cups
- Sugar - 2 Tablespoons
- Ground Ginger - 1/2 Teaspoon
- Brown Sugar - 1/2 Cup
- Flour - 1/2 Cup
- Rolled Oats - 3/4 Cup
- Cinnamon - 1 Tablespoon
- Melted Butter - 1/2 Cup

Directions:

1. To begin, put your blueberries into a half size foil pan and spread them out evenly.

2. Mix your sugar and ground ginger and evenly coat all the blueberries.

3. Mix the remaining ingredients together and distribute evenly over the top of the blueberries.

4. Bring your AKORN Kamado up to 375 degrees with a chunk of cherry wood for smoke and the Smokin' Stone in place to set up for indirect cooking.

5. Once the smoke is a clean smoke, that is thin and blue, place your half steamer pan on the AKORN for forty minutes. After forty minutes remove from AKORN, let cool and enjoy.

Faux Apple Pie

Ingredients:

- 3 Cups Almond Flour (Crust)
- Baking Powder - 3 Tbsp (Crust)
- 1/3 Cup Xanthan Gum (Crust)
- 1/2 Cup and 1 Tbsp Coconut Flour (Crust)
- Apple Cider Vinegar - 2 Tbsp
- 3 Eggs, Whisked (Crust)
- Water - 3 Tbsp (Crust)
- 6 Chayote Squash, peeled, cored, sliced thin (Filling)
- 1 Cup Lakanto Golden Sweetener (Filling)
- Cinnamon - 2 Tbsp (Filling)
- Nutmeg - 1 tsp (Filling)
- Vanilla - 2 Tbsp (Filling)
- Lemon Juice - 3 Tbsp (Filling)
- 1/4 Cup Lankanto Classic Granulated Sweetener (Filling)
- Butter - 3 Tbsp (Filling)
- 1 Bag Cinnamon Pecan Lollis Cookie Clusters (Topping)

Directions:

1. Mix all wet ingredients in one bowl, set aside.

2. Mix all dry ingredients in large bowl, once dry ingredients are combined, slowly add were ingredients.

3. Mix with a spoon as good as you can, then knead with hands.

4. Shape into a ball, wrap in saran wrap and refrigerate for 2 hours.

5. Combine in a sauce pan, cook over medium heat for 20 minutes.

6. Add more sweetener if desired.

7. Remove from heat to cool.

8. Roll out dough between 2 sheets of parchment paper until 1/4 inch thin, place in aluminum pie pan - trim edges.

9. Poke holes in crust with fork.

10. Preheat grill to 325-350°.

11. Place pie crust on grill over indirect heat.

12. Cook about 5-8 minutes until crust starts to turn golden.

13. Remove from grill, add pie filling and even spread the crumbled Lollis Cookie Clusters over the top until filling is covered.

14. Place pie back on grill over indirect heat for about 25-30 minutes until nicely browned.

15. Let pie cool completely before serving.

16. Pairs well with vanilla Rebel Creamery ice cream.

Guinness Cupcakes With Whiskey Salted Caramel Buttercream

Cooking Time: 25 Min

Ingredients:
- 1 Devils food Cake Mix
- 1 3.9 Oz Instant Chocolate Pudding
- 1 Cup Sour Cream
- 1/2 Cup Guinness
- 1/2 Cup of Oil
- 4 Eggs
- 3/4 Cup Mini Chocolate Chips
- 1 Cup of Light Brown Sugar
- 1/4 Cup of Butter
- 1/4 Cup of Milk
- 1/4 Cup of Whiskey
- 1/4 Tbsp Sea Salt
- 4 Sticks of Unsalted Butter
- 6 Cup of Powdered Sugar
- 1/4 Cup of Salted Caramel

Directions:

1. Heat Akorn to 325 for indirect heat and add liners to a cupcake pan Add cake mix, pudding, sour cream, oil, Guinness, eggs, and ½ c. of the chocolate chips in a large bowl and mix together until combined Divide batter evenly into 24 cupcakes Bake for 20 minutes or until middle of the cake springs back when gently pushed down or until a toothpick inserted into the center comes out clean While cupcakes are cooling, add brown sugar, 1/4 c. butter, milk, and sea salt to a medium sauce pan On medium heat, melt caramel mixture stirring frequently until mixture starts to simmer Allow to simmer without stirring for 5-7 minutes until thickened. Remove from heat and allow to cool To make the frosting, add butter to mixer and beat until smooth and creamy. Slowly add the powdered sugar and beat until light and fluffy. Add caramel to frosting and beat until combined Top cooled cupcakes with a spoonful of buttercream and spread across the cupcake I like to add a drizzle of the leftover caramel on top of the frosted cupcakes with a little sprinkle of the leftover chocolate chips

2. If caramel starts to thicken too much to drizzle, you can microwave it for 10 seconds

OTHER FAVORITE RECIPES

Bacon Cinnamon Rolls

Cooking Time: 8 To 10 Min

Ingredients:

- Can of Cinnamon Rolls
- 8 Slices of Bacon

Directions:

1. Heat AKORN with Smokin' Stone and drip pan to 350 degrees.
2. Grease an 8 or 9 inch round pan.
3. Open the can of cinnamon rolls and separate the rolls.
4. Unroll the Rolls.
5. Cook bacon on grill until crisp but still flexible.
6. While bacon is still warm, places two slices of bacon on top of 1 unrolled cinnamon bun and roll bun back up.
7. Repeat steps for other rolls.
8. Place cinnamon rolls in pan and cook until golden brown.
9. Top with icing and serve warm.

Smoked Sweet Potatoes

Cooking Time: 20 Min

Ingredients:

- (5) Sweet Potatoes or Yams
- Olive Oil
- Himalayan Pink Salt
- Thai Spice
- Sugar Free Maple Syrup
- Maple Cinnamon Seasoning
- Butter

Directions:

1. Start by venting the potatoes with a fork Brush EVOO on the potatoes, fully covering them Sprinkle with Himalayan pink salt Heat your grill to 300° Put the smoking stone in place Place your potatoes around the grill so they get indirect heat (This allows them to cook and absorb the smoke flavor without burning) Add a flavor chunk Flip the potatoes at the 1 hour mark Pull the potatoes when they are soft and have some give when you press in on them (Be careful as these will be extremely hot) Open the potatoes down the middle (Again, use caution as they will be hot) Use a fork to mix in Thai spice seasoning with the potato Add a dollop of butter and let it melt
2. Sugar Free Maple Cinnamon Butter
3. stick of butter, salted and soft SF Maple Syrup, 1/4 cup Maple Cinnamon Spice, 2 TBSP

Flat Iron 3-step Breakfast Sandwiches

Cooking Time: 10 Min

Ingredients:

- 4 English Muffins
- 4 Eggs
- 4 Sausage Patties (optionally combine ground pork with herbs and spices of your choice and salt and pepper to prepare homemade patties)
- 4 Slices Of Cheese Or 1 Cup Of Shredded Cheese
- Any Condiments Of Your Choice

Directions:

1. Heat Flat Iron to medium-high heat. Cook sausages (or ham) for 2-3 minutes per side in one

section and fry eggs in another section. Once you have space, toast each english muffin split in half and face down on the flat top. Assemble each sandwich with english muffin to start, spreading any condiments then stacking one sausage, one fried egg and cheese in between. Serve warm, enjoy.

Garlic Bacon Green Beans

Cooking Time: 20 Min

Ingredients:

- 1 Pound Fresh Green Beans, Ends Trimmed
- 1/2 tsp Salt
- 1 Tbsp Olive Oil
- 1 Tbsp Butter
- 8 Garlic Cloves, Minced
- 6 Strips of Bacon, Cooked and Chopped

Directions:

1. Prepare charcoal grill for direct medium-high heat.
2. Fill a large pot more than halfway with water. Bring to boil.
3. Add green beans (water should cover all the beans), and salt. Cook for 5 minutes on medium heat then drain the beans.
4. Heat olive oil and butter in a large skillet over medium-high heat coals.
5. Add minced garlic, constantly stirring, for about 30 seconds.
6. Add cooked bacon and green beans. Saute on medium-high heat for about 1-2 minutes stirring to combine. Remove from heat.
7. Serve immediately and enjoy!
8. Optional topping: Toasted Sliced Almonds

Sweet Potato Medallions

Cooking Time: 30 Min

Ingredients:

- 1 Large Sweet Potato, 1/2 inch slices
- Olive Oil
- 4 oz. Goat Cheese
- 1 Tbsp Heavy Cream
- 1 Tbsp Honey
- 1 Tbsp Dried Cranberries, Chopped
- 1 Tbsp Walnuts, Chopped
- 1 tsp Fresh Thyme, Chopped

Directions:

1. Light grill for indirect heat and heat grill to 375 degrees
2. Brush both sides of the sweet potato slices with olive oil
3. Sprinkle them with cinnamon and sugar on both sides
4. Place slices directly on grill or on a mesh cooking tray
5. Allow the slices to cook for 15 minutes then turn over and cook for an additional 15 minutes
6. Mix together goat cheese, cream, and honey in a small bowl
7. Spoon a teaspoon of the cheese mixture on the warm sweet potato slices
8. Sprinkle each slice with cranberries, thyme, and walnuts
9. Drizzle with honey before serving

Honey Mustard Chicken

Cooking Time: 35 Min

Ingredients:

- 2-3 Lbs Split Chicken Breast
- 1/4 Cup Honey
- 1/4 Cup Mustard
- 1 Tsp Kosher Salt
- 1/2 Tsp Coarse Black Pepper
- 1/4 cup Honey

- 1/4 Cup Mustard
- 2 Tsp Apple Cider Vinegar
- 1 Tsp Worcestershire Sauce
- 1/2 Tsp Hot Sauce

Directions:

1. Trim any excess fat off the chicken and place in a container with the marinade mixture consisting of honey, mustard, salt, and pepper. Let chicken marinate for 3 or more hours.

2. When ready to cook prepare the grill to a temperature of 375 F. Remove excess marinade from the chicken and place indirectly on the grill.

3. Create your honey mustard sauce in a heat resistant bowl by adding honey, mustard, apple cider vinegar, Worcestershire sauce, and hot sauce. Bring to a boil and let simmer.

4. Once chicken has reached an internal temp of 160-162 F brush on the honey mustard sauce and let the chicken continue to cook till internal temperature is 165 F

5. Pull the chicken off the grill at internal temperature of 165 F. Serve and enjoy!

Maple Bourbon Rubbed Stuffed Chicken Breasts

Cooking Time: 20 Min

Ingredients:

- 6 Chicken Breasts
- Sea Salt To taste
- Maple Bourbon Rub, To Taste (Or Your Favorite Chicken Seasoning)
- 3 Sweet Peppers (Diced)
- 1 Jalapeno (Diced)
- 1/2 White onion (Diced)
- 1/2 Cup Mozzarella Cheese (Shredded)

Directions:

1. Step 1 - Dice peppers and onions and brown in skillet, set aside

2. Step 2 - Shred cheese, set aside

3. Step 3 - Tenderize each chicken breast with a fork, pay dry

4. Step 4 - Season with salt and let the chicken sweat for a few minutes, stuff with peppers and cheese and season chicken breasts

5. Step 5 - Heat grill up to about 450° ~ place chicken on grill and cook to an IT of 165°. Make sure to toss in a chunk of cherry for that nice smokey flavor

6. Step 6 - Pull, let rest and serve with some pan sheet veggies or a salad

Grilled Apple Strudel

Cooking Time: 30 To 45 Min

Ingredients:

- 4 Granny Smith Apples
- 1 Cup Brown Sugar
- 1 Cup Golden Raisins
- 1 Sheet Frozen Puff Pastry, Thawed
- 1 Egg
- 1/4 Cup Milk

Directions:

1. Preheat grill to 400 degrees F (200 degrees C).

2. Line a baking sheet with parchment paper.

3. Peel, core and slice 3 apples. Peel, core and shred 1 apple. Place all prepared apples in a large bowl.

4. Stir in brown sugar and golden raisins; set aside.

5. Place puff pastry on baking sheet and roll lightly with a rolling pin.

6. Arrange apple filling down the middle of the pastry lengthwise. Fold the pastry lengthwise around the mixture.

7. Seal edges of pastry by using a bit of water on your fingers, and rubbing the pastry edges together.

8. Whisk egg and milk together, and brush onto top of pastry.

9. Bake on the grill for 35 to 40 minutes, or until golden brown.

Smoked Bacon-brisket Bbq Beans

Cooking Time: 4 Hrs

Ingredients:

- Brown Sugar Baked Beans- 85 Ounces
- White Beans- 15 Ounces
- Pinto Beans- 15 Ounces
- Kidney Beans- 15 Ounces
- Canned Diced Tomatoes- 28 Ounces
- Cooked Brisket- 2 Hefty Handfuls
- Large Sweet Onion- 1
- Minced Garlic- 1 Clove
- Vegetable Oil- 1 Tablespoon
- Beer- 1/2 Cup
- Garlic Powder- 1 Tablespoon
- Brown or Stone Ground Mustard- 2 Tablespoons
- White Vinegar- 1/4 Cup
- Louisiana Hot Sauce- 2 Tablespoons
- Bacon- 1 Pound

Directions:

1. Start by preparing your AKORN or favorite Char-Griller smoker for indirect heat at 275°f. I prefer using applewood for this recipe but use your favorite wood. I've done these beans with mesquite, cherry, and also hickory and they have always turned out great.

2. Set burner to med-high heat and pour vegetable oil into skillet. Saute chopped onion and minced garlic to slightly soften and brown. Set aside.

3. Slice uncooked bacon into 2" bite sized squares (Pull out entire pound of bacon slices and cut all at once) Set aside.

4. Pour assorted beans into large mixing bowl. Add your diced tomatoes. Combine remaining ingredients (minus the bacon) into the bowl and stir until all ingredients are evenly mixed with beans.

5. Pour contents into large baking pan. Lay bacon over top of beans piece by piece, rooftop style. Once the beans are covered, if you end up with extra bacon pieces, build a second layer around the outside and work your way inward toward the middle.

6. I like to sprinkle a little extra Char-Griller Rib Rub or Pepper on the rooftop bacon but this is optional.

7. Once smoker is running steady around 275°f place beans inside and let the magic happen!

8. Check every hour. Cook Time for these beans averages about 3 ½ hours- 4 hours. You are looking for the top to have a dark rich mahogany color, a caramelized look, and rooftop bacon should be fairly firm.

9. Let beans rest 10-15 min to slightly cool before eating!

Flavor Pro™ Smoked Turkey Breast

Cooking Time: 2 Hrs

Ingredients:

- 3 Lb All Natural Turkey Breast Roast
- 2 Tbsp Onion Powder
- 2 Tbsp Garlic Powder
- 1 Tbsp Paprika

- 1 Tbsp Chili Powder
- 1 Tbsp Parsley
- 1 1/2 Tsp Black Pepper
- 1 Tbsp Paprika

Directions:

1. Rinse off your turkey breast roast and pat dry with a paper towel. (Leave the netting on, you will cut that off at the end of the cook) Spray on a coat of olive oil cooking spray. Generously apply all the ingredients or salt-free seasoning to all sides of the turkey breast roast. Place the seasoned turkey in the refrigerator for 15 minutes while your grill heats up. Prepare your Flavor Pro for indirect heat at 275°f by filling the far left slot and the middle slot of the Flavor Drawer with charcoal. Add a few chunks of smoking wood to the coals as well. I used hickory for this recipe but feel free to use whatever smoking wood you like. Use both burners on the left to light the charcoal. Once charcoal is lit, you may turn your burners off. Keep both smoke stacks open. Use a water pan for this recipe. Feel free to use water, apple juice, or a mixture. Place pan on the far right slot of the Flavor Drawer underneath the grate. Once your Flavor Pro is up to temperature, add your turkey breast roast to the far right side of the grill grate, away from the heat source and directly above your water pan. Add more coals or wood as needed to maintain your temperature. Smoke for approximately 2 hours or until your turkey reaches an internal temperature of 165°f. Start temperature probing your turkey around an hour of cooking time. Be sure to keep a close eye on the internal temperature, going over 165°f can cause your turkey to dry out. Let rest for 15 minutes. Cut of netting with scissors then slice. Enjoy!

Lemon Pepper Wings

Cooking Time: 45 Min

Ingredients:

- 2-3Lb Chicken Wings & Drums
- 1.5 Tsp Dried Lemon Zest (Approx. 5 Lemons)
- 1 Tsp Kosher Salt
- 1 Tsp Coarse Black Pepper
- 1.5 Tsp Garlic Powder
- 1.5 Tsp Onion Powder
- 1 Tbsp Olive Oil
- 6 Tbs Butter
- 1.5 Tsp Coarse Black Pepper
- 1 Tsp Fresh Lemon Zest (Approx. 1 Lemon)
- 1 Lemon (Juiced)

Directions:

1. Collect lemon zest from approximately 5 lemons. Bake lemon zest in an oven on lowest setting until it has completely dried out (20-30 minutes). In a small shaker combine dried lemon zest, 1 Tsp black pepper, ½ garlic powder, ½ onion powder.

2. Apply a 1 Tbsp of Olive oil onto the wings to help act as a binder for the rub. Generously coat the wings on all sides with the lemon pepper rub.

3. Heat grill to 375 F. Place chicken wings on the grill once the grill has reached desired temperature.

4. In a heat safe bowl combine butter,1 ½ black pepper, 1 Tsp fresh lemon zest, and the juice of 1 lemon. Bring the mixture to a boil and reduce heat to let simmer.

5. Once the chicken has reached an internal temp of at least 165 F you can remove from the grill and place in a large bowl. Toss the wings in the lemon pepper sauce mixture. Serve and enjoy!

Jalapeño Bacon Blanket Poppers

Cooking Time: 30 Min

Ingredients:

- 4 Jalapenos
- Char-Griller Steak Rub to Taste
- 1/3 Cup Cream Cheese
- 3 Slices of Bacon
- Shredded Cheese to Taste

Directions:

1. They came out perfect and he can't wait to make them again. It was quick, easy and delicious. He used the AKORN Jr to make these as it is the perfect size grill/smoker for these type of appetizer cooks and the grill will burn all day making it easy to make more during the game if you run out!
2. Mix cream cheese, shredded cheese, Char-Griller Steak Rub in a bowl and set aside.
3. Slice jalapeños through the middle to make it boat shaped.
4. Using a spoon remove the pith and seeds to create room for the filling.
5. Tip: If you like heat then leave some seeds behind. Seeds provide the heat.
6. Fill jalapenos with filling.
7. Slice bacon into small strips then lay it over the filling on the jalapenos.
8. Sprinkle a small portion of the Char-Griller Steak Rub on top of the bacon.
9. Fire up your Char-Griller Grill to 400°.
10. James used his AKORN Jr & Smokin' Stone with Fogo Charcoal Premium Lump Charcoal and FOGO Starters to ignite it.
11. Place Jalapeño Bacon Blanket Poppers in the grill/smoker and smoke for 30 minutes or when the bacon is golden brown.
12. Remove and enjoy!

Smoked Bone-in Pork Shoulder Steak

Cooking Time: 2 Hrs

Ingredients:

- Bone-in Pork Shoulder Steaks (1 1/2 to 2 in. thick) - 2
- Char-Griller Rib Rub- To Your Tasting
- Cranberry Juice - 1/2 Cup
- BBQ Sauce - 1/2 Bottle
- Apple Wood/Charcoal

Directions:

1. Season both sides of the pork steaks liberally with Char-Griller Rib Rub. Set aside and to allow the steaks to marinate. Begin prepping the fire to 275 F. *Tip* Put a water pan inside your smoker to allow for extra moisture.
2. Once the smoker has reached 275 F put the pork steaks onto the grill and let the smoker do the work.
3. Around the 45-minute mark pull the steaks and wrap individually with foil and add ¼ of the cranberry juice to each foil packet. Put back on the smoker at 275 F.
4. Once the steaks reach around 198 F take them out of the foil packet and sauce with your favorite BBQ sauce. Put back in smoker for another 10 minutes to let the sauce settle.
5. Pull the steaks from the grill and let rest for 10 minutes. Serve and enjoy!

Smoked Buffalo Chicken Wing Dip

Cooking Time: 3.5 Hrs

Ingredients:

- 1 Small Chicken (4 to 6 lbs)
- 1/2 Cup Char-Griller Chicken Rub

- 1 Can of Beer
- 1/3 Cup Veggie Cream Cheese
- 1/3 Cup Blue Cheese Dressing
- 1/3 Cup Buffalo Sauce
- 1 tsp Garlic Powder
- 1/2 tsp Salt
- 1/2 tsp Pepper
- Celery, Carrots, Baguette, Crackers For Dipping

Directions:

1. From Aubrey: I don't know who needs to hear this, but SMOKED CHICKEN BELONGS IN BUFFALO CHICKEN DIP! It's football season, and if you're a fan of the games, or a fan of the snacks (hello, it's me), this smoky twist will truly take your tailgating to the next level. Let's dig in.

2. Fill a chimney with charcoal, and 3-4 small pieces of mesquite. Light, and let coals get hot. Add to smoke box, and adjust the air-flow to a small flow to ensure temperatures sit right around 275.

3. Rub chicken with Char-Griller Chicken Rub, and "stand up" on beer can. Place in smoker, close lid, and let smoke for 3 hours, until chicken is done and has reached 165 internal degrees. Let cool, then shred.

4. Preheat oven to 375, and mix 1.5 cups shredded chicken with cream cheese, blue cheese dressing, buffalo sauce, garlic powder, and salt & pepper.

5. Transfer to an oven safe dish, and bake for 20 minutes, until golden brown and bubbly.

6. Serve with your favorite items for dipping. Enjoy!

Red Pepper Eggs

Cooking Time: 15 Min

Ingredients:

- Red Pepper Sliced as Rings (3/4in. Thick) - 2
- Eggs - 2
- Precooked Bacon, Crumbled - 5-7 Slices
- Shredded Pepper Jack Cheese - 1/4 Cup
- Butter
- Salt and Pepper - To Taste

Directions:

1. Preheat grill to 350 degrees and place skillet on heat

2. Melt butter (1-2 Tbsp) and cook red pepper slices for 4-5 mins per side to soften

3. Crack eggs directly into pepper rings, season with salt and pepper and close lid for another few minutes (longer for a more well-done egg)

4. After egg has cooked, sprinkle with pepper jack cheese and bacon crumbles. Serve for a yummy breakfast of champions!

Char Grilled Wings

Cooking Time: 20 Min

Ingredients:

- Chicken Wings - 2 to 4 Pounds
- Hot Sauce - 1/2 Cup
- Melted Butter - 1/4 Cup
- Salt - 1 Tablespoon
- Hot Sauce (for Sauce) - 1/2 Cup
- Minced Garlic (for Sauce) - 2 Cloves
- Cayenne - 1 Teaspoon

Directions:

1. If you're like my family, you're counting down the days to football season. That means tailgates at the stadium, or in your own backyard, and if you've got the cute transportable AKORN Jr,

Grilled Wings are absolutely in your tailgating future.

2. I do my wings a little differently, I like to soak them in plain old cayenne vinegar hot sauce for 48 hours before I grill them. This is 100% optional, but I'm telling you- the flavor profile is unreal. Add a few hunks of Applewood to your charcoal while grilling these for a flavor explosion. Pro Tip: Baste your wings in the sauce at the very end to keep them from burning. Since they marinated in the hot sauce for hours, the flavor is packed in. Let's dig in.

3. After rinsing and drying your wings, toss in hot sauce, avocado oil, and salt. Marinate for 24-48 hours.

4. When you're ready to grill, add a few chunks of Applewood to your charcoal, and get the grill nice and hot. Oil your grates and spread the wings out evenly. Grill on each side for 8 minutes, until crispy and golden brown.

5. While the wings finish cooking, brush the buffalo sauce over each side, and turn 1-2 more times to allow the sauce to caramelize. Dip them in your favorite ranch or blue cheese, and enjoy!

Flat Iron Portobello Bun Burgers

Cooking Time: 10 Min

Ingredients:
- 1 Lb Ground Beef
- 1 Tbsp Onion Powder
- 1 Tbsp Garlic Powder
- 1 Tbsp Worcestershire Sauce
- 1/4 Cup Minced Garlic
- Salt and Pepper
- 6-8 Portobello Mushroom Caps
- 2 Tbsp Of Olive Oil
- Cheese Slices Of Your Choice
- Your Favorite Burger Toppings

Directions:

1. In a bowl, mix ground beef, onion powder, garlic powder, minced garlic, salt and pepper, and Worcestershire sauce. Shape into burger patties. Heat a zone to your Flat Iron to medium heat. Add olive oil and mushroom caps. Cook for about 3-4 minutes on each side. Remove from heat and set to the side. Add burger patties and cook for about 5 minutes per side to desired doneness. Add cheese to burgers and allow them to melt. Assemble burgers with one mushroom cap, the burger and any additional toppings, then top with another mushroom cap. Serve hot. Enjoy!

Maple-dijon Grilled Chicken Sandwich

Cooking Time: 15 Min

Ingredients:
- 1 Lb chicken breast (Cut In Half Lengthwise and Then In Half Again)
- 1/2 Lb Sharp Cheddar Slices
- 1/2 Lb Sharp Cheddar Slices
- 1 Medium Apple (Sliced Thin)
- 1/4 Cup Red Onion (Sliced Thin)
- 1/4 Cup Fresh Cilantro (Leaves Only)
- 1/4 Cup Olive Oil
- 1/4 Cup Red Wine Vinegar
- 2 T Maple Syrup
- 1 T Dijon Mustard
- 1 Tsp Salt
- 1/2 Tsp Pepper
- 4 Burger Buns (Brioche or Any Choice)

Directions:

1. Preheat your Char-Griller to high heat. Scrape grates clean and spray with a high-heat non-stick spray.

2. Combine oil, vinegar, maple syrup, mustard, and salt in a jar, and shake till combined. Pour half of the dressing over the chicken and let it marinate while your grill heats up!

3. Next, add greens, cilantro, onion, and apple slices to a large bowl

4. Take marinated chicken to the grill. Grill on each side for 3 mins. Since the chicken is a thin cutlet, cook time is quicker! Once the chicken is cooked through on both sides, turn off the heat, and add slices of cheese to each piece. Close the grill and let cheese melt for 1-2 mins. Toast your buns at this time, too.

5. Pull chicken and buns from the grill, toss your salad with the remaining dressing, and pile your toasted buns with 2 pieces of the chicken, and a handful of salad. These sandwiches go perfectly with sweet potato fries for the Ultimate Fall dinner! Enjoy!

Flat Iron Tomato Soup Grilled Cheese

Cooking Time: 8 Min

Ingredients:

- 8 Slices of Bread (Your Favorite Kind)
- 4 Slices of Cheese (Your Favorite Kind)
- 2 Tomatoes (Cut Into 8 Slices)
- 8 Leaves of Fresh Basil
- 1 Tbsp of Garlic Salt
- 1 Tbsp of Olive Oil

Directions:

1. Drizzle bread with olive oil, and sprinkle slices with garlic salt. Arrange on Flat Iron Griddle, and let the bread begin to toast for 2 minutes.

2. Next, layer your Slice of bread with cheese, slices of tomato, and basil. Arrange the rest of the ingredients on the bread and the cheese to melt, about 5 more minutes.

3. Fold opposite half onto it's match, and pull sandwiches from Griddle. Cut in half, and enjoy!

Easy Grilled S'mores

Cooking Time: 5 Min

Ingredients:

- 4 Whole Graham Crackers Split Into Halves (8 Total)
- 4 Jumbo Marshmallows
- 2 Chocolate Bars
- Aluminum Foil

Directions:

1. If not already fired up, preheat the grill to medium heat. Arrange 4 aluminum foil packets, with one fully assembled s'more per packet (one chocolate square and one marshmallow per 2 graham cracker squares.) Grill each packet for about 5 minutes or until the marshmallows are melted. Additionally, you can only put the chocolate and graham crackers in the foil alone and individually roast marshmallows on a skewer for that delicious charred taste prior to layering on your s'more. Serve immediately, enjoy!

Grilled Pineapple

Cooking Time: 4 Min

Ingredients:

- 1 Fresh Pineapple, cored and sliced
- 3 Tbsp of Melted Butter
- 1/2 Tsp of Hot Sauce
- Kosher salt to taste

- 1 Tsp of Honey

Directions:

1. In a large bowl or bag, combine pineapple slices with honey, butter, hot sauce and salt. Allow to marinate for an hour through overnight. Heat grill to high, direct heat. Grill pineapple slices for 3-4 minutes per side, allowing grill marks to form. Serve with the desired dish. Enjoy!

Fabulous Buttermilk Pancakes

Cooking Time: 4 Min

Ingredients:

- 2 Cups All Purpose Flour
- 1 Tsp Baking Soda
- 1 Tsp Salt
- 1 Tablespoon Sugar
- 1 Egg
- 3 Cups Buttermilk

Directions:

1. Preheat part of your griddle to 375°-400° Mix well all the dry and ingredients Mix the buttermilk into the dry ingredients, it's ok if lumpy. In a separate bowl, crack the egg and whisk it incorporating air into the egg until it is light and bubbly. Eggs that are not straight out of the refrigerator will whip up easier. Add the egg to the other ingredients and mix, JUST to incorporate. DO NOT OVERMIX Grease the area of the griddle for pancakes with vegetable oil Drop approximately 1/2 cup plus a little bit more of the batter onto the hot griddle and let it spread out. Cook until the bottom side is golden brown. Flip pancake and lightly brown. Serve with butter and warm maple syrup. Enjoy these light fluffy pancakes

Smoked Salmon

Cooking Time: 1 Hrs

Ingredients:

- 1 Salmon Fillet
- 1 Tsp of Sea Salt
- 1 Tsp of Black Pepper
- 2 Tsp of Mustard or Dijon Mustard
- ½ Tsp of Old Bay Seasoning
- 1 Lemon(Sliced)

Directions:

1. Instruction
2. Preheat the smoker to 225 degrees by adding a fruity wood like apple or cherry to your Side Fire Box Don't own a Side Fire Box? Not to worry. Simply arrange wood in your barrel on the outside of your cooking area/opposite the area you plan to cook your fillet on. If you plan to cook your salmon on the left side of the grates, arrange the wood under the right, and so on. Lightly coat the flesh side of salmon with mustard, then season with salt, pepper and Old Bay seasoning. Place in smoker and lay slices of lemon on top of salmon until internal temperature of salmon reaches 140 degrees (should take about 1 hour depending on type and size of fillet) Remove from smoker and let rest for at least 10 minutes before slicing Serve warm, enjoy!

Flat Iron Sundried Tomato Omelet

Cooking Time: 10 To 15 Min

Ingredients:

- 2 to 3 Eggs
- 2 Tbsp Milk
- 1 Tbsp Sundried Tomatos

- 1 to 2 Slices Diced Ham
- 1/8 Cup Mozzarella Cheese, Shredded
- Fresh Basil, Chopped
- Salt and Pepper to Taste

Directions:

1. Whisk together eggs, milk, and salt and pepper

2. Preheat griddle to medium high and add desired oil

3. Pour egg mixture on griddle using the spatulas to make sure it doesn't spread too much.

4. Allow to cook for 2 to 3 minutes and add in tomatoes, cheese, ham and basil to one side of the omelet and use the spatula to fold over the other side to make the omelet.

5. Turn down the burner to medium low and allow to cook until cheese is melted, flipping once.

Butternut Squash Soup

Cooking Time: 45-50 Min

Ingredients:

- 1 large butternut squash, halved and seeded
- ½ C. chopped shallot
- 1 Tsp. salt
- 4 garlic cloves, minced
- 1 Tsp. maple syrup
- ⅛ Tsp. ground nutmeg
- Freshly ground black pepper, to taste
- 3-4 C. vegetable broth
- 1-2 Tbsp. butter
- 1-2 Tbsp. heavy whipping cream
- Olive oil

Directions:

1. Pre-heat the grill to 425°F. Rub 1 Tsp. of olive oil over the inside of both halves of the squash and sprinkle with salt and pepper. Wrap each half in foil, adding a ½ C. water to each. 2. Place on the grill and bake for 45-50 minutes, until squash is tender and completely cooked through. Remove from grill and allow to cool for 10 minutes. Unwrap, and use a large spoon to scoop the flesh into a bowl, discarding the skin. 3. In a large soup pot over medium heat, add olive oil and chopped shallot and sauté until the shallot has softened, 3-4 minutes. Add garlic and cook until fragrant, about 1 minute, stirring frequently. 4. Transfer the cooked shallot and garlic to a blender. Add the squash, maple syrup, nutmeg and freshly ground black pepper, to taste. Slowly add vegetable broth and blend until creamy. 5. Add 1- 2 Tbsp. heavy whipping cream to taste, and blend well. Taste and blend in more salt and pepper, if needed.

2. Serve immediately. Let leftover soup cool completely and refrigerate for up to 4 days or freeze for up to 3 months.

Smoked Beer Can Chicken Recipe

Cooking Time: 2.5 Min

Ingredients:

- 1 Whole Chicken (4-5 Lbs)
- 3 Tbsp of Extra Virgin Olive Oil
- 2 Tbsp of Salt
- 2 Tsp of Black Pepper
- 2 Tbsp of Dry Rub of Choice
- 1 Can of Beer of Choice

Directions:

1. Combine seasonings and spices in a bowl to prepare the ultimate rub for chicken. Coat the entire chicken with olive oil then season(including the cavity) with the rub and store the remainder in an airtight container for a future cook. Preheat the smoker to 225-275 degrees by adding desired coals to your Side Fire

Box If you do not own a Side Fire Box, you can still enjoy the smoking experience. Simply arrange coals opposite of where you plan to place the chicken. If you will sit the chicken in the middle of the grill, arrange coals on the perimeter, and so on. Pour out (or drink!) ¼ to ½ of the can of beer. Place the chicken at the center of the grill on top of the beer can with the chicken legs and beer can holding it up. Close the smoker and allow chicken to cook until internal temperature reaches 165 degrees (around 2 hours). Remove chicken and wrap in aluminum foil or butcher paper, allowing to rest for at least 20 minutes before carving. Serve warm, enjoy!

Grilled Watermelon Salad

Cooking Time: 10 Min

Ingredients:
- Watermelon - Small
- Feta - 4 oz
- Mint - 1 Bunch
- Basil - 1 Bunch
- Limes - 2
- Balsamic - 2 Tbs
- Red Onion - 1 Sliced
- Olive Oil - 3 Tbs
- Salt - 1 tsp

Directions:

1. Slice red onion and place in a bowl of ice water. Leave submerged for 10 minutes. 2. Slice the end off each side of the watermelon. Stand watermelon on its end. Slice the rind off. 3. Cut watermelon into slices. 4. Brush Watermelon with olive oil and set aside. 5. Preheat charcoal grill to medium and oil the grates. 6. Grill the watermelon slices until they are just marked. About 2 minutes on each side. 7. Set aside to cool. 8. In a bowl, whisk together olive oil, balsamic, lime juice, and salt. 9. Roughly chop the mint leaves and basil. 10. Cut watermelon into chunks, add to a bowl. 1 Add feta, herbs, and dressing. Toss gently. 12. Serve right away and enjoy.

Garlic & Herb Seasoned Potatoes

Cooking Time: 10 Min

Ingredients:
- 3-4 Large Russet Pot
- 1/3 Cup Olive Oil
- 1 Tsp White Whine Vinegar
- 1 Tbs. Spicy Mustard
- 2 Tsp. Chargriller Garlic & Herb Seasoning
- 3 Garlic Cloves (Minced)
- 4 Tbs Melted Butter
- Parsley To Garnish

Directions:

1. Put your Char-Griller Garlic & Herb seasoning to delicious use beyond just meat with these Garlic & Herb seasoned potatoes.

2. Steam potatoes in pressure cooker for 5 minutes.

3. While that's cooking combine all the other ingredients listed above.

4. Once finished, drain in colander and place in bowl.

5. Pour mixture over potatoes while they are still warm and give them a good toss. Add salt and pepper to taste.

6. Top with parsley and enjoy with your next meal.

Bbq Fiends Chicken Lollipop Recipe

Cooking Time: 45 To 60 Min

Ingredients:

- Chicken Drumsticks - 2 lbs
- Char-Griller Chicken Rub 1/4 Cup
- BBQ Sauce of Choice - 3/4 Cup
- Apple Juice - 1/4 Cup
- Honey - 1 tsp
- Tiger Sauce - 1 tsp
- Coarse Black Pepper - 1 tsp

Directions:

1. With your boning knife cut where the chicken starts to thin out going towards the joint. Cut all around the bone and use a paper towel to help with the removal of the skin and joint. Push the meat down towards the thick end of the drumstick to form the lollipop presentation.

2. Tip: You will notice tendons and a little bone that runs parallel to the leg after you have cut it. Make sure to remove these with your boning knife or kitchen shears.

3. Once all your drumsticks have been trimmed and free of tendons it is time to wrap the exposed bones in foil (this will help with presentation so you don't end up with burnt bones).

4. Tip: During this step I usually start my fire prep by lighting my charcoal chimney.

5. Next, use your seasoning and apply liberally to your lollipops. Make sure to get as even as a coat as possible.

6. For chicken lollipops, grill with indirect heat because you are looking to keep them moist and without char marks. Pour your charcoal chimney into one half of the grill and adjust air ducts.

7. Get your grill up to 325 F.

8. Add oak chunks as well just to give the meat an extra layer of flavor.

9. Once grill is up to temp arrange your chicken lollipops so they are standing up on the half of the grate that is not above the flame.

10. Tip: While your grill is coming up to temp you can refrigerate your chicken to help the seasoning process and to firm up the chicken a bit more. I find this helps with them standing up in lollipop form.

11. Let the grill do its work.

12. Start preparing the glaze by combining BBQ sauce, apple juice, honey, tiger sauce, and black pepper in a microwavable safe cup. Set aside till it is time to glaze.

13. Tip: I always warm my sauce right before it is time to glaze so that it is smooth and doesn't tack on to the meat too heavily. Microwave for 1 to 1 1/2 minutes right before you glaze.

14. Once your chicken has reached internal temp around 165 F, it is time to glaze.

15. Dip each chicken lollipop into the cup with your glaze mixture until you have obtained a nice shine.

16. Quickly put the chicken back on the grill and let the internal temp reach 170 F.

17. At this point you will pull the chicken off the grill and dip in the glaze again if needed.

18. Put on a platter and cover loosely with foil. Let rest.

19. Once the chicken has rested for about 10 minutes it is time to impress your family and friends.

20. Take that foil off and let the crowd be in awe of your creation! I promise they will be even more impressed once they get a taste!

Easter Brunch French Toast

Cooking Time: 8-10 Min

Ingredients:

- 2 thick slices of Challah bread
- 5 strips of bacon
- 6 eggs (3 for frying)
- 1 C. heavy cream
- ¼ C. milk
- 1 Tsp. cinnamon
- Juice of ½ lemon
- Butter as desired for skillets
- Pinch of salt, optional
- Maple syrup, for serving
- Fresh berries, optional, for garnish

Directions:

1. Fry bacon in a cast iron skillet to desired crispness according to package directions, drain grease and wipe pan. Set aside on a plate and keep warm. 2. While bacon is frying, add 3 eggs to another skillet and prepare as desired, scrambled, sunny side up, etc. Cover and keep warm. 3. Beat remaining eggs in a medium bowl and add heavy cream, milk, cinnamon, lemon juice and a pinch of salt, if desired. Whisk until well blended. 4. Dip Challah bread in mixture, making sure to evenly coat both sides and add to hot cast iron skillet. 5. Cook for 2-3 minutes on each side until golden brown.

2. To serve, top French toast with maple syrup and fresh berries.

Cowboy Steak With Asparagus And Onion

Cooking Time: 1½ Hrs

Ingredients:

- Cowboy Steak
- 1 bunch asparagus, ends trimmed
- 1 onion, sliced
- Steak BBQ Rub, to taste
- Original All-Purpose BBQ Rub , to taste
- Garlic butter
- Sea salt, to taste
- Olive oil

Directions:

1. #TeamCharGriller Ambassador James Llorens took innovation to the next level with this Cowboy Steak recipe. He decided to use the Char-Griller Rotisserie Kit as an innovative way to reverse sear the steak. After letting it reach 130°F, he took it off the Rotisserie and seared it off on the Char-Griller AKORN.

2. Asparagus and onions round out this impressive meal and Lloren's Garlic Butter recipe adds that final finishing touch to make the steak shine.

3. Using a sharp knife, make a small hole at the end of the bone so it can fit in the rotisserie fork.

4. Apply olive oil, sea salt and Steak BBQ Rub to both sides of the Cowboy Steak.

5. Tip: Do not add sea salt or rub/seasoning to the bone to avoid it from burning while roasting.

6. Place the Cowboy Steak in the rotisserie forks and set aside. Place two forks in the meat and one fork in the bone hole.

7. Season asparagus and onions with Original All-Purpose BBQ Rub and set aside.

8. Pre-heat the Char-Griller Super Pro™ 2121 to 300°F. Place the rotisserie with the Cowboy Steak and onions in the grill/rotisserie motor.

9. Tip: Make sure the charcoal is more on the meat side of the rotisserie versus the bone side.

10. Tip: Prop up the grill lid halfway using the grate lifter.

11. While your Cowboy Steak is roasting pre-heat the Akorn Kamado 6719 and cook your asparagus. Once the asparagus is done allow the grill to get extremely hot to sear Cowboy Steak.

12. Tip: Place a chimney starter in the center of the Kamado for extreme direct heat in the middle of the grill.

13. Roast the Cowboy Steak to 130°F or your desired temperature using the folding probe thermometer. Remove from the steak from the grill and remove the steak completely off of the rotisserie forks. Let rest for 5-10 minutes then apply the melted garlic butter to both sides.

14. Tip: Spray canned olive oil/vegetable oil on the grates to avoid the steak sticking to the grates.

15. Transfer the steak to the Kamado for 1-2 minutes on each side. Remove the steak from the grill and allow to rest for 10-15 minutes. Slice the steak and sprinkle on sea salt.

16. Plate the onions, asparagus and Cowboy Steak and serve with A1 Steak sauce for additional flavor, if desired. Enjoy!

Smoked Mac And Cheese

Cooking Time: 1-2 Hrs

Ingredients:

- 6 Tbsp of Butter
- 1/3 Cup of Flour
- 3 Cups of Milk
- 6 Cups of Shredded Cheese of your choice
- Kosher Salt
- Black Pepper
- 2 Tsp of Paprika
- 4 Cups of Elbows, Macaroni, cooked
- 1 tsp of Cayenne Pepper

Directions:

1. Preheat the smoker to 225-250°F. Heat a large cast iron skillet to medium heat on your stove. Add butter and allow it to thoroughly melt. Whisk in the flour until bubbly and thoroughly combined. After 2-3 min, pour in the milk stirring constantly until the sauce thickens. Add 4 of the 6 cups of cheese, stirring until thoroughly combined and melted. Mix in the seasonings then add elbows to the cheese sauce. Once thoroughly combined, sprinkle the remaining 2 cups of cheese over the top. Place the skillet into your smoker and allow it to cook uninterrupted for 1-2 hours depending on how intense you'd like the smoky flavor. Allow to rest for 5-10 minutes then serve immediately. Enjoy!

Chicken Fajita Quesadillas

Cooking Time: 20 Min

Ingredients:

- 3 Chicken Breast (Cut in Half)
- 1 Yellow Onion (Thinly Sliced)
- 1-2 Bell Peppers (Thinly Sliced)
- 2 Cups Cheddar Cheese (Freshly Grated)
- 6 Medium Tortillas
- 1 Tsp Ground Cumin
- 1 Tsp Ground Chili Powder
- 1 Tsp Garlic Powder
- 1 Tsp Salt
- 1 Tsp Pepper
- 2 Tbl Olive Oil or Avocado oil

Directions:

1. Heat your Char-Griller Flat Iron Gas griddle to medium heat, and spread avocado oil across the surface with tongs and a towel.

2. Turn the first section to high heat. Toss chicken breast in cumin, chili powder, garlic, salt,

& pepper. Lay chicken on first section, over high heat, and cook 4 minutes per side.

3. Add onions and peppers to Flat Iron, and cook over medium until softened and cooked through.

4. After flipping the chicken breast, finally add the tortillas to the Flat Iron Griddle, and sprinkle evenly with cheese. Add a cooked chicken breast to each tortilla and a serving of the peppers & onions, folding each tortilla over the filling in half to make a moon shaped quesadilla.

5. Serve as is, or with a side salad. Enjoy!

Supreme Grilled Portobello Pizza

Ingredients:
- 1-4 Portobello Mushroom Caps
- 2 Tbsp Olive Oil
- 2 tsp Garlic Powder
- 1/2 Cup Pizza Sauce
- 1 Cup Shredded Mozzarella Cheese
- 1/2 Cup Cooked Sausage Crumbles
- 1/4 Cup Green Pepper, Chopped
- 1/4 Cup Onion, Chopped

Directions:
1. Scoop out the gills and cut out the stem of the portobello mushroom cap and brush with a mixture of olive oil and garlic powder.
2. Grill for 10 minutes at 425 degrees.
3. Top each with sauce, cheese, sausage, peppers and onions, return to grill for another 10 minutes. Serve!

Flavor Pro Bacon Wrapped Jalapeño Poppers

Cooking Time: 20 To 25 Min

Ingredients:
- 10 Jalapeno Peppers
- 1 (8 oz) Package of Cream Cheese, Softened
- 1 Package of Shredded Cheddar Cheese
- 20 Slices of Thin Cut Bacon
- 1/2 tsp Chipotle Powder
- 1/2 tsp Garlic Powder
- Salt and Pepper to Taste

Directions:
1. Halve the jalapeños and clean out all the seeds.
2. Mix together the cream cheese, 1 cup of cheddar cheese, chipotle powder, garlic powder, salt and pepper.
3. Fill the pepper halves with cream cheese mixture.
4. Wrap the peppers in strips of bacon.
5. Set up the Flavor Pro for direct cooking
6. Add 20 to 30 charcoal briquettes to the flavor drawer
7. Ignite charcoal with gas burners set to medium high
8. Once charcoal is lit, turn off gas burners and allow to fully ash over.
9. At this point, you can add a handful of soaked wood chips if desired.
10. Place wrapped jalapeños on grill for 20 to 25 minutes or until bacon is crispy.
11. Remove from grill and serve.

Grilled Lemon Pepper Potatoes

Cooking Time: 20-25 Min

Ingredients:
- 1 Lb Of Russet Or Red Potatoes (Sliced Or In Cubes)
- 1/2 Tbsp Of Garlic Powder
- Extra Virgin Olive Oil
- Salt
- Char-Griller "Lemon Pepper" Rub

Directions:

1. Preheat your grill to high heat. In a bowl, toss potatoes with a generous amount of olive oil, garlic powder, salt and desired amount of salt and the Char-Griller "Lemon Pepper" Rub. Place potatoes in a foil packet. Fold it to cover the food and twist the edges to seal it close. Place on your grill and cook for 20-25 minutes or until desired tenderness or crispiness., ensuring to mix/flip potatoes midway through.

Flat Iron Pineapple Coconut Pancakes

Cooking Time: 15 Min

Ingredients:

- 1 1/2 Cup of All-Purpose Flour
- 2 Tsp of Baking Powder
- 1 Tsp of Baking Soda
- 1/4 Cup of Sugar
- 1/2 Tsp of Salt
- 2 Large Eggs
- 1/4 Cup of Butter (Melted)
- 1 Tsp of Butter or Cooking Spray for Griddle
- 1 Cup of Crushed Pineapple
- 1 Cup of Shredded Coconut (Ground Finely)
- 1/4 Cup of Coconut Milk

Directions:

1. In a large mixing bowl, prepare the batter by stirring together baking powder, baking soda, sugar, salt, eggs, butter, crushed pineapple, coconut, and coconut milk. Slowly add flour until you achieve a nice batter, not too runny and not too thick. Mix until it is smooth with no lumps.

2. Heat the Flat Iron over Medium-High Heat and spray with cooking spray or melt butter. Pour pancake batter onto griddle with amount depending on desired size of pancakes.

3. When lots of bubbles form on top, flip over and cook the other side until lightly browned.

4. Serve warm and drizzle with honey or maple syrup.

Loaded Grilled Radish Bites

Cooking Time: 25 Min

Ingredients:

- 6 Large Radishes, Washed and Halved
- 2 Tbsp Butter
- 1 Tbsp Herb & Sea Salt Blend
- 1/4 Cup Shredded Cheddar Cheese
- 1/4 Cup Sour Cream
- 2 Slices Bacon, Crumbled
- 1 Tbsp Finely Chopped Fresh Chives

Directions:

1. Melt butter and combine with herbed sea salt. Pour over radishes in a bowl and toss to coat.

2. Lay the radish halves over a wire rack and grill at 425 for 20 to 25 minutes, or until tender.

3. Top with cheese, dollops of sour cream, crumbled bacon, and chives.

Smoke Roasted Coffee

Cooking Time: 15 Min

Ingredients:

- 1/2 Pound Green Coffee Beans

Directions:

1. Light a single chimney of charcoal and get it entirely lit.

2. Drop that down into our AKORN and start adding some smoking chips to the fire. You can use whichever smoke wood you like, today we are going to go with white oak.

3. Get yourself a cast iron skillet, today I'm using an 8 inch model, a whisk, a colander, and

some green coffee beans. Now that you're all set put the skillet on the grill grate and let it get hot. Once it is warmed up go ahead and add as many coffee beans to it that you feel you can stir and continuously agitate, for us that's gonna be about half a pound.

4. From here on out just focus on stirring the beans and about every minute close your lid for 10 or so seconds to let those beans soak in that smoke. After about 15ish minutes you should start hearing the first crack, it'll sound like popcorn. If you want a lighter roasted coffee you can take your beans off now but for a more medium roasted coffee let it keep going until you hear a second round of cracking.

5. At this point you want to cool your beans down immediately. We're going to do this by tossing them in a colander.

6. Tossing them does two things, one is it helps the beans cool more quickly and the other is as the beans are tossed in the air the husks will float off and not remain in our coffee beans.

7. From this point you just need to set your beans aside loosely covered for a day so they can off-gas and finish the process.

8. After that grind them up , make coffee your favorite way and prepare to have some of the best coffee you've ever had, and you made it all yourself on the grill.

9. Let me know how it works out for you and till next time, y'all take it easy.

Cheddar Jalapeño Chicken Burgers

Cooking Time: 20 Min

Ingredients:

- 1 Package Of Ground Chicken
- 1/2 Cup Of Yellow Onion
- 1 Tbsp Of Cilantro
- 1 Tbsp of Parsley
- 2 Tbsp Of Minced Garlic
- 2 Tbsp Of Finely Chopped Jalapeno
- 1 Tsp Of Cumin
- 1 Tsp Of Black Pepper
- 1 Tsp Of Paprika
- 1/2 Cup Of Cheddar Cheese (Tiny Cubes or Shredded)
- 1 Tbsp Of Sea Salt
- Lettuce
- Mayonnaise As Needed
- Sliced Red Onions
- 4-6 Burger Buns

Directions:

1. In a medium bowl, combine the ground chicken, garlic, onion, jalapeño, cheese, and all seasonings and spices. Mix thoroughly using your hands, but be sure not to over ground the meat. Form patties of your desired thickness and size. Cook the burgers on your preferred grill over medium-heat, ensuring they are thoroughly cooked before serving, given it is a poultry product. Serve patties on a burger bun, topped with mayo, lettuce, onions, and any other desired condiments.

Grilled Flank Steak With Vegetables

Cooking Time: 20 Min

Ingredients:

- 1.5 Pound Flank Steak
- Smoked Paprika - 1.5 tsp
- 2 Garlic Cloves, Minced
- Salt and Pepper to Taste
- 4 Ears of Corn

- Two Large Zucchini, Cut in Half Lengthwise
- 1 Pint Cherry Tomatoes
- Olive Oil - 3 Tbs
- 1.5 Tbs Fresh Rosemary, Chopped
- Red Wine Vinegar - 1 Tbs
- 2 Garlic Cloves, Minced (Oil Dressing)
- Canola Oil - 2 Tbs

Directions:

1. Season flank steak with paprika and garlic. Rub on all sides and season with salt and pepper. Brush with canola oil.

2. Brush corn, zucchini, and tomatoes with canola oil and season with salt and pepper.

3. Preheat grill to medium high heat.

4. Add flank steak to grill, flip once and cook to desired doneness. About 4 to 6 minutes per side, let rest 5 minutes.

5. Add vegetables to grill and turn occasionally until lightly charred all over.

6. Whisk olive oil, rosemary, red wine vinegar, garlic and salt and pepper to taste in a small bowl.

7. Brush steak and drizzle vegetables with olive oil mixture and serve with steak immediately.

Fresh Chili Lime Watermelon Fries

Cooking Time: 5 Min

Ingredients:
- 1 Seedless Watermelon
- 2 Tsp of Tajin Chili Lime Seasoning
- 1 Tsp of Sea Salt
- 1 Cup Greek Yogurt
- 1/2 Fresh Squeezed Lime
- 1/2 Tsp of Chili Powder
- 1 Tbsp Honey

Directions:

1. Slice the watermelon into long, "french fry" formation. Combine the sea salt, and chili lime seasoning in a large bowl. In a separate bowl, combine yogurt, lime juice, chili powder, and honey. Mix thoroughly. Serve the yogurt mixture alongside the watermelon for easy dipping.

Smoked Butternut Squash Soup

Cooking Time: 1 Hrs

Ingredients:
- 1 Butternut Squash
- Sea Salt
- Coconut Oil
- Fresh Rosemary
- 1 Onion
- Vegetable Broth

Directions:

1. Split a butternut squash down the middle and scoop out the seeds. Give it a little layer of coconut oil and top with sea salt. Add a stem of fresh rosemary to each side and put it on the grill. You're going to want to get your grill at about 300°. Place the squash on there to smoke until the flesh is easily manipulated with a fork (about an hour). Remove from grill. Slice up an onion and sautee it in a pan over medium. Add half the pan to a blender, 5 cups of vegetable broth and 1 side of the squash (with rosemary pulled from the stem). Blend on high until everything looks blended. Salt and pepper to taste. Repeat with the other squash and onions. Serve and enjoy!

Super Pro Rotisserie Prime Rib

Cooking Time: 180 Min

Ingredients:

- Prime Rib: Two Bones (6 Pounds)
- Olive Oil
- Char-Griller Grills Chili Lime: to taste.
- Sazon: to taste.
- Brazilian Salt: to taste
- Fresh Parsley Flakes or Fresh Cilantro Flakes: to taste. Used Cilantro. You can also use dry flakes if fresh is not available.
- Kitchen Twine
- Char-Griller Grills Super Pro & Rotisserie Kit
- Fogo Eucalyptus Lump Charcoal

Directions:

1. Rinse and pat dry the prime rib. Trim access fat and skin. French cut the bones with a knife. Apply coating of olive oil to all sides. Season all sides with Sazon, Chili Lime seasonings and Brazilian Salt. Add kitchen twine in the middle of the bones on the meat and knot. Add to rotisserie rod and lock in using the rotisserie forks. Then Sprinkle fresh parsley or cilantro flakes. Heat grill with lump charcoal: When coking over an open fire I don't cook at specific temperature. I begin with an equivalent of a ½ chimney full of lump charcoal and monitor the fire by feel. I place the charcoal in the middle of the grill in the back. As the charcoal burns I add pieces as the cook goes along. Place rotisserie in the grill. Roast until internal 115°. Remove from the grill. Allow to rest for 15 minutes. Slice and enjoy!

Alabama White Sauce

Cooking Time: 3 Min

Ingredients:

- 2 Cups Mayonnaise
- 1/3 Cup Horseradish
- 2 Tsp Dijon Mustard
- 1/3 Cup Apple Cider Vinegar
- 2 Tbsp Lemon Juice
- 1/4 Tsp Minced Garlic
- 1 Tsp Sea Salt
- 1 Tsp Black Pepper
- 1/2 Tsp Cayenne Pepper
- 1/2 Tsp Oregano Flakes
- 1/2 Tsp Garlic Powder

Directions:

1. Alabama White Sauce is a creamy, tangy, with just a pinch of heat.

2. Combine all the ingredients together in a medium bowl. Whisk until the mixture is creamy. Store in an airtight container and refrigerate until ready to use.

Shrunken Head Apple Punch

Cooking Time: 45 Min

Ingredients:

- 7 Small Apples
- 1/2 Cup Orange Juice
- 6 Cups Apple Juice
- 2.5 Cups Pineapple Juice
- Juice of 1 Lemon
- 1/4 Cup Honey
- 1/4 tsp Pumpkin Spice
- 2 Cinnamon Sticks

Directions:

1. Light grill for indirect heat and heat to 225.

2. Peel apples.

3. Carve little eyes and mouths into the apples with a tip of a butter knife.

4. Place remaining ingredients in a shallow pan.

5. Place apples on grill along with the pan.

6. Allow to smoke for 45 minutes.

7. Remove pan and apples from grill and allow to cool.

8. Transfer juice to a punch bowl and add in apples.

Ale Chicken Drumsticks

Ingredients:

- Drumsticks- 14
- Ale of Choice- 3 ounces
- Char-Griller Chicken Seasoning- 2.5 Teaspoons

Directions:

1. Soak for an hour in 3 oz of ale of choice

2. Rub down with 5 teaspoons of Char-Griller chicken seasoning

3. Smoke uncovered for and hour on an aluminum foil sheet at 250°F, wrapped in foil until done

Teriyaki Chicken And Mango Skewers

Cooking Time: 10 To 12 Min

Ingredients:

- Teriyaki Sauce - 1 Bottle
- Boneless, Skinless Chicken Thighs - 4 Pounds
- 3 Mangos
- 1 Large Red Onion
- Sesame Seeds - For Garnish
- Salt and Pepper - To Taste
- Chopped Scallions - For Garnish

Directions:

1. Cut chicken thighs into 1-inch cubes and place in a bag with the teriyaki sauce.

2. Refrigerate overnight.

3. Peel and cut the mango into 1-inch cubes.

4. Preheat the grill to medium high heat.

5. Add the mango and chicken to the skewers.

6. Grill the skewers covered for 10 to 12 minutes, turning occasionally.

7. Remove from the grill and rest.

8. Sprinkle with sesame seeds and scallions.